Come, You Taste

MINNESOTA
HISTORICAL
SOCIETY PRESS

Come, You Taste

FAMILY RECIPES FROM THE IRON RANGE

B. J. CARPENTER

www.mnhspress.org
The Minnesota Historical Society Press is a member
of the Association of American University Presses.

Manufactured in the United States of America

9-23-16   10 9 8 7 6 5 4 3 2

∞ The paper used in this publication meets the minimum requirements
of the American National Standard for Information Sciences—
Permanence for Printed Library Materials, ANSI Z39.48–1984.

International Standard Book Number
ISBN: 978-0-87351-969-4 (paper)

LIBRARY OF CONGRESS CATALOGING-IN-PUBLICATION DATA
Carpenter, B. J., author.
Come, you taste : family recipes from the Iron Range / B.J. Carpenter.
pages cm
Includes bibliographical references and index.
ISBN 978-0-87351-969-4 (paperback)
1. Cooking, American—Midwestern style. 2. Cooking—Minnesota. 3. Iron ranges—Minnesota—Social life and customs. I. Title.
TX715.2.M53C395 2015
641.59776—dc23
2015025607

* * *

Cover illustration: Tetyana Kulikova/123RF

*To all the immigrant great-grandparents and grandparents,
mothers and fathers, friends and neighbors,
who are the Iron Range.
Thank you.*

CONTENTS

With the passage of years the proportion
of immigrants in the Mesabi population has
steadily diminished. In 1900, half the residents were
foreign born; in 1940, the proportion had dropped
to twenty per cent, as indicated by the federal census
of that year. The immigrants and their children,
however, constitute eighty-five per cent of the total
population. Today the American-born children
of the immigrants are the adults of the Mesabi
communities, and they carry on after their parents.
From twenty-five to thirty-three per cent of these
immigrant young have intermarried with members
of other minority groups. The range is actually
a melting pot, and by the time a third generation
appears there, the ethnic identity of most of its
members will be obscure or unimportant. Interest
in ancestry will then be more one of curiosity
than of concern with ethnic origins.

JOHN SIRJAMAKI,
THE PEOPLE OF THE MESABI RANGE, 1940

Come, You Taste

INTRODUCTION
An Entrusted Legacy

I'm a chef and writer by schooling, and my primary language is "food," something I come by as a native second-generation Iron Range resident. I hold fond memories of the foods and gardens, languages and traditions provided and tended by my immigrant neighbors and grandparents, and I know I'm not alone. During every manner of ex-pat Iron Range gatherings—weddings, funerals, family and class reunions, even pickup hockey games in winter—at some point the conversation always, and I mean always, turns to the food we ate growing up. With more than forty different nationalities doing the cooking, our menu options were limitless.

I'm always astonished when nieces, nephews, children of friends, the next generation—many who were born on the Range, and some who still live there—tell me they aren't familiar with, or have never even tasted, many of the foods that were part of their parents' and grandparents' common language. The importance of this subject had been simmering in the back of my brain for twenty or thirty years, and with my decades-long background in food I felt it my duty to try to remedy this sad situation.

Not long after I began writing this book in earnest, I came to realize it had already been documented—in an oral sense—by the people whose story it is, and how lucky I am to have been a beneficiary of such a rich legacy, shared and taught by those generous immigrants. I'm just a grateful medium whose charge is to commit to paper their stories, often in the words of their colorful assimilated language, and to help preserve and push forward something essential that is in danger of being left behind.

. . .

Give me your tired, your poor,
Your huddled masses yearning to breathe free,
The wretched refuse of your teeming shore.
Send these, the homeless, tempest-tost to me,
I lift my lamp beside the golden door!
EMMA LAZARUS, 1883

These last lines of Emma Lazarus's poem, written one year after the first shipment of iron ore left the sparsely populated area that would become known as Minnesota's Iron Range, might be viewed as a mandate from the Sleeping Giant—*Missabe*—the name given to the territory by its native Ojibwe inhabitants. For nearly fifty years after Lazarus penned those lines, thousands of poor immigrants would pass her iconic verse, inscribed at the foot of the Statue of Liberty, en route to Minnesota in response to the need for workers generated by the discovery of iron ore, and in hope of a better life.

In the 1860s, rumors of a possible mother lode of gold that might rival and possibly eclipse deposits uncovered in California a few years earlier drew prospectors to an area near Lake Vermilion in northeastern Minnesota. Though the rumor of gold remained a rumor, the prospectors' efforts were rewarded. The cache of red hematite running through the veins they opened sparked an iron mining boom that would surpass California's seven-year gold rush by nearly ten decades.

More than forty different nationalities faced uncertain lives when they first arrived on the Iron Range at the start of the twentieth century. Confronted with unfamiliar situations and surrounded by multitudes of people whose customs, faiths, and languages were different from theirs, they instinctively did what was needed to survive. Collectively gathering with fellow countrymen, they formed neighborhoods and alliances, places of support, safety, and comfort where the needs of their families could be met. Taking care of family was foremost, and at the top of the list of priorities was food, a commonality shared by all. Everyone had to eat.

Potica/kolache; sarma/braciole; lutefisk/baccala; fattigman/lefse; zuppa inglese/trifle. This disparate-sounding group of words—more alike than meets the American ear—embodies some of the beloved everyday and special occasion dishes that once graced the tables of these first Rangers. Early in the twentieth century some of the only places these foods might be found outside of immigrant kitchens were in the lunch pails carried by the miners and the numerous ethnic social clubs established in the mining locations and villages. Three or four different languages might be spoken in some neighborhoods and on some streets, and numbers of children born in the United States started school unable to understand what their teachers and some of their classmates were saying. In time they would learn to speak English and bring their lessons home, often becoming teachers to their parents, who would begin to talk to their neighbors, communicating over backyard fences and gardens, sharing fruits and vegetables, trading recipes and stories. Food was a language everyone understood.

The majority of first-generation Iron Rangers were born between the onset of World War I and the stock market crash of 1929 that ended the living-large days of the Roaring Twenties. Growing up during and surviving the hardships of the Great Depression, these hardscrabble kids came of age right around the start of World War II. By this time many of the language and social barriers that had existed among these diverse communities had fallen to the wayside through school interactions and cross-cultural marriages. Over the years, aided by guidance from their immigrant parents, these firstborn citizens managed to keep family dishes and customs alive through the 1960s and into the early 1970s. The inevitable passing of this first generation, compounded with a diminishing awareness and interest among successive generations, places these important food traditions in great danger of disappearing. Not only are recipes being lost; family, cultural, and socioeconomic histories are all at risk.

Come, You Taste chronicles this history with the daily meal pattern typical of the time, one that reads differently from the present day. It begins with breakfast, followed by dinner—the midday meal; supper—eaten in the early evening; and lunch—typically served in the mid-evening around eight or nine o'clock when there was company. Afternoon coffee, often shared with neighbors, was between dinner and supper, and usually included one of the hostess's sweet specialties. Family recipes and stories celebrating the foods eaten every day and on holidays and traditional occasions are here for you to enjoy.

I hope this culinary record will engage readers and encourage future descendants to embrace and carry forward this important legacy entrusted to them by Minnesota's first Iron Rangers.

CHAPTER 1

Breads

There is religion
in a good loaf of bread!

MRS. WANNER OMAN,
THE CHISHOLM AMERICAN JUBILEE BICENTENNIAL COOK BOOK

9 chose to start this book with a chapter on bread because it is the most basic and most universal of foods, eaten in most societies, at nearly every meal. Bread has sustained people for thousands of years, crossing all cultures and faiths through millennia. From the early Romans to Judeo-Christians, Hindis to neo-pagans, the breaking of bread has been a symbol of both sustenance and salvation; a universal communion at every family table.

Some cultures, the Scandinavians in particular, favored a rounded shape with a hole in the center for the express purpose of storage. Once baked, the loaves were slid onto a pole which was suspended from the root cellar ceiling, the goal being to sustain the family through the long winter and well into the beginning of summer, when new spring wheat was ready to harvest. To this day the traditional shape for Swedish hardtack is a thin, dimpled round, about twelve inches in diameter, with a large hole in the center.

The daily breads of the Slavs got their start when small amounts of whole grains and seeds were placed in a dish along with dried beans and the seeds for other essential crops and set on a table or dining room sideboard at Christmas, where they were blessed and would remain until

Epiphany. The dish was stored until spring, when the blessed seeds would be mixed with others before planting. Slavic breads were heavy and dense, made from multiple flours, with wheat—*šenica*—for the foundation, in combination with other nutritious whole grains like barley—*ječama*—and spelt—*pir*. The loaves were usually leavened with a good yeast "start" or *kvass,* one that had often been shared between neighbors for years.

Bread was essential; in times of financial insecurity it was something most people could afford. The ingredients were basic and usually available, and it was easy to produce. Before commercial bakeries were commonplace, bread was made at home in big batches—typically once a week or sometimes monthly depending on the size of the family—and baked in wood-burning ovens. Baking in such quantity required the help of the whole family. Young children were brought to the table to help mix the flours and, when old enough, to knead the heavy mounds of dough. Nothing beat a slice of fresh-baked bread, still warm from the oven, topped with homemade jelly and butter—if your family was lucky enough to own a cow. To keep large numbers of loaves fresh for an extended time, bread was stored in tight-lidded tin cans or bread boxes or in basements or cool, dark root cellars.

Every crumb from every loaf was accounted for and used. Dried ends and stale rusks became milk toast for the sick, pabulum for teething babies, and a panacea for the elderly, whose teeth were gone or nearly so. English and Cornish immigrants revived stale loaves with something called vinegar pudding, the French sliced stale baguettes into croutons to add thickness to soups, the Germans and Slovenians used sweetened crumbs inside strudel (page 142) or to coat pastries, and the Italians' incorporation of stale, dried pieces as a salad ingredient resulted in the peasant classic and now chic, upscale bread salad (page 115).

Holiday, special occasion, and everyday recipes—some with multiple steps and directions, others simple and straightforward—are included, with a few historical notes and profiles kneaded in for good measure.

GREAT AUNT NELLIE ANDERSEN'S WILD BLUEBERRY MUFFINS

[makes 12 muffins]

Of five sisters, my great-aunt Nellie was the baker, a skill fostered by her mother as she grew up in Goodland, just southwest of Nashwauk, and honed during her married years, which were spent in Chicago. Every summer for a week or ten days, she returned to the Iron Range, where two sisters and a brother remained on the family farm, and her visits always seemed to coincide with wild blueberry season. She'd been an avid blueberry picker, another skill born out of a rural childhood where roadside ditches were thick with patches that seemed to go on for miles, and there were no wild blueberry patches in Chicago.

For several days of her visit, a few great-nieces and -nephews were enlisted to comb the ditches near Goodland, a task willingly taken on; the more blueberries we picked, the more muffins we'd eat.

*If using frozen fruit in baking, never thaw before incorporating into the mixture; the juice will "bleed" into the dough or batter. Tossing fruit—both fresh and frozen—in flour to lightly coat before adding will prevent this; always add fruit after the flour and liquids have been combined.

STREUSEL TOPPING

½ cup white sugar

⅓ cup all-purpose flour

½ teaspoon cinnamon

4 tablespoons (½ stick) salted butter, chilled and cubed

FOR MUFFIN TINS

1 tablespoon salted butter, at room temperature

2 teaspoons cinnamon mixed with 2 teaspoons white sugar

BATTER

4 tablespoons (½ stick) salted butter, at room temperature

⅓ cup white sugar

1 large egg, beaten

1 teaspoon vanilla

2¾ cups all-purpose flour, divided

½ teaspoon salt

1 tablespoon plus 1 teaspoon baking powder

1 cup whole or 2 percent milk

1½ cups fresh or frozen* wild blueberries

ANGEL FOOD CAKE.
SIFT FLOUR AND SUGAR ← not together
BEFORE MEASURING. USE
UNGREASED 10 INCH TUBE
PAN.

1 1/4 C SIFTED CAKE FLOUR
1/2 C SIFTED SUGAR
1 1/2 C EGG WHITES (ABOUT 12)
1/4 TSP SALT
1 1/4 TSP CREAM OF TARTAR
1 TSP VANILLA
1/4 TSP ALMOND EXTRACT
1 1/3 C SUGAR

Measure sifted flour, add 1/2 c sugar - sift 4 times. Combine egg whites, salt, cream of tartar, and flavorings in a large bowl.

large bowl. Beat with large spoon until moist soft peaks form. Add the rest of sugar in 4 additions beating until blended each time.
Sift in flour mixture in 4 additions folding in with spoon. Turn bowl often.

Bake at 375°
35 to 40 min.
Invert pan on rack til cool. Then loosen from sides with knife
Good Luck - Aunt Nellie.

1. Preheat oven to 375 degrees. To make the topping, in a medium bowl, combine sugar, flour, and cinnamon; cut in cold butter with a fork or rub with your fingertips until evenly mixed; set aside. Grease muffin cups with softened butter, and sprinkle each with cinnamon-sugar to coat inside; tap excess into the bowl with the streusel topping. Set pan aside.

2. For the batter, in a large bowl, use an electric mixer to beat 4 tablespoons butter and sugar until fluffy; add beaten egg and vanilla and mix well. Sift 2 1/4 cups flour onto a flexible cutting board or a piece of waxed or parchment paper; resift with salt and baking powder. Starting and ending with dry ingredients, add to the butter-sugar mixture alternately with milk. Sprinkle remaining 1/2 cup flour over blueberries, toss to coat, and gently fold into batter.

>>

3. Fill muffin cups two-thirds full and sprinkle tops with streusel mixture. Bake for 20 to 25 minutes, until an inserted wooden pick comes out with a few crumbs that are moist, not wet; tops should be lightly browned and crackled. Serve warm.

Cook's Notes: *Remove the muffins from the pan to a cooling rack as soon as you take them out of the oven; this will keep the outsides coated with the cinnamon-sugar. Serve with butter.*

SIX-WEEK REFRIGERATOR BRAN MUFFINS

[makes 72–96 muffins]

The origin of these muffins is somewhat unclear. I found the faded, typewritten recipe on a very fragile, multiply folded, stained piece of paper among a number of my grandmother's recipes, most of which were on cards in her handwriting; and she didn't type. I do remember she made bran muffins quite often, and with seven boys to feed, this was probably the recipe she used. I've made them; it works!

. . .

For moist, healthy, and freshly baked bran muffins every morning, try these. This recipe makes a very large quantity of batter that holds for up to six weeks in the refrigerator in a tightly sealed glass or stainless container. Soaking two of the six cups of bran and refrigerating immediately after mixing helps the batter keep its texture. Preheat the oven first thing in the morning and before you start the coffee, scoop chilled batter into greased or paper-lined muffin tins. Serve warm, with creamed honey or unsalted butter.

6 cups whole bran cereal (buds, not flakes)

2 cups boiling water

1 cup canola oil

4 large eggs

1 cup packed brown sugar

4 cups buttermilk

zest and juice of 1 orange

2 cups all-purpose flour

5 teaspoons baking soda

2 teaspoons salt

2–2½ cups total, alone or in combination: raisins, dried cranberries, finely chopped dates, chopped unpeeled apples, or toasted walnuts, optional

1. Preheat oven to 400 degrees. Place 2 cups bran buds in a large bowl and cover with boiling water; let stand for 5 minutes. Mix in canola oil and let stand for another 5 minutes.

2. In a separate bowl, beat eggs and whisk in sugar; add buttermilk, orange juice and zest, and remaining 4 cups of bran. Sift flour, baking soda, and salt into a medium bowl; add dried fruits and/or nuts (if using), and stir to coat with flour mixture. In three steps, alternately combine sugar-buttermilk mixture and dry mixture with soaked bran, stirring well after each addition. Scoop desired amount into greased or paper-lined muffin tins, no more than two-thirds full; bake for 20 minutes.*

3. Remove from muffin tins, allow papered muffins to cool for a few minutes, and serve warm.

Cook's Notes: *These are great for Christmas and other cold-weather brunches. Include the dried cranberries; substitute tangerine zest and juice for orange and slightly toasted slivered almonds for the walnuts. Serve with whipped cream cheese in place of honey or butter.*

*While muffins are baking, store remaining batter in a glass or stainless steel container that has a tight-fitting lid. Refrigerate for up to six weeks.

MRS. MCGUINNESS'S
GINGER-RHUBARB SCONES

[makes 16 small scones]

My grandmother was born here near the end of the nineteenth century, to first-generation English parents, about the same time as Mrs. McGuinness, her neighbor across the road out in the country, had been born in Scotland. Mrs. McGuinness came to America as a postwar bride; her husband went to work in the mines. By the late 1950s both women were widows, but their more common bond was a mutual respect for proper British ritual, upheld with many teas shared across the road over the years.

Mrs. McGuinness's were the first scones I ever had, and they became the ruler by which all others in my life would be measured. Maybe it was because she'd scurried across the road with them one bright June morning in the very early 1960s, the treats wrapped in a tea towel, just out of the oven and still warm. It was a Monday. I remember because school was out for the summer, and I'd come after church the day before to stay with my grandmother for a few days. We ate them at the picnic table under the budding lilacs, the hint of delicate scent about to emerge no competition to the aroma of those scones dusted with ginger sugar and studded with little bits of rhubarb, the first of the season. They were delicious.

. . .

"Employing a quick, light hand is the secret to properly made scones. They should be flaky, buttery, and eaten while still warm, at their *very* best," proclaimed Mrs. McGuiness when she arrived with her offering. "And they should be served with a knob of the freshest butter."

I daresay she was right, because hers were every bit the way she said they should be, down to the last crumb caught among the threads of my grandmother's handmade lace tablecloth. I still remember the light flaky texture and the taste of sour rhubarb as it came against the heat of the ginger, both quelled by the granules of sugar that skim-coated the top and the large knob of butter I'd slathered on before I bit in.

Mrs. McGuinness's other imperative: "It's important all ingredients be at room temperature." She was right about that, too.

2 cups all-purpose flour	1 large egg, at room temperature, beaten
1 teaspoon baking soda	½ cup buttermilk, at room temperature
2 teaspoons baking powder	
1 teaspoon salt	3 tablespoons half-and-half or whole milk
2 teaspoons ground ginger	
2 teaspoons white sugar	1½ teaspoons ground ginger mixed with 1½ teaspoons white sugar
½–¾ cup minced rhubarb	
3 tablespoons salted butter, at room temperature	

1. Preheat oven to 375 degrees. Lightly grease and flour a baking sheet. Measure flour by dipping the cup into the container; don't pack. In a large bowl, stir together flour, baking soda, baking powder, and salt. In a smaller bowl, combine 2 teaspoons ginger, 2 teaspoons sugar, and minced rhubarb; stir to coat. Add to flour and stir well to combine.

2. Work the butter into the flour mixture with fingertips until coarse crumbs form. Stir beaten egg into buttermilk, and quickly work into flour-butter mixture, tossing with fingers just until combined. Turn out onto a floured surface, and knead *as little as possible* to bring dough together into a soft, pliable ball. Cut into 4 equal pieces with a slightly wet kitchen knife or metal spatula. Use your knuckles to flatten each into a 6-inch circle about ½ inch thick.

3. Transfer to prepared baking sheet; prick the surfaces with the tines of a fork. Cut each into quarters with the wet knife, separate slightly; brush with half-and-half and sprinkle with ginger-sugar. Bake for 15 minutes or until just light brown; bottoms should be pale tan. Remove from oven to a basket or plate lined with a cloth napkin, and serve warm.

Cook's Notes: *Substitute toasted walnut pieces for rhubarb and nutmeg for ginger, or use in combination, adjusting amounts. Currants are the classic addition to scones, but any small dried fruit like cherries, cranberries, or blueberries are good, too. These freeze well but are best right out of the oven.*

SWEDISH RUSKS

[makes 27 rusks]

These slightly sweetened biscuits are sometimes referred to as "Scandinavian biscotti" for their striking resemblance to the Italian counterpart baked in the same manner. The Swedish version is flavored with cardamom instead of anise and eaten dunked in coffee instead of wine. Traditionally they are moistened with warm milk and given to teething babies or made into a lovely milk toast for the ill and the elderly.

• • •

Rusks keep well if allowed to dry—usually overnight—and stored in tightly covered tins. Bake several batches at a time to have on hand for unexpected company or to give as hostess gifts.

16 tablespoons (2 sticks) salted butter, at room temperature

1 cup white sugar

2 large eggs

1 tablespoon heavy cream

¾ teaspoon pure almond extract

3 cups all-purpose flour

>>

| 1 teaspoon baking powder | ½ teaspoon salt |
| ½–¾ teaspoon ground cardamom | ⅛ teaspoon baking soda |

1. Preheat oven to 350 degrees. Grease 3 small (e.g., 5¾ x 3 x 2–inch) loaf pans. In a large bowl, beat butter and sugar; stir in eggs, cream, and almond extract. Combine dry ingredients (flour through baking soda), and gradually add to butter-sugar mixture; batter will be thick.

2. Spoon into prepared pans. Bake for 35 to 40 minutes, until a wooden pick inserted near the center comes out clean. Cool in pans for 10 minutes.

3. Remove breads to a cutting board. With a serrated knife, shave off end crusts in very thin slices; set aside to make crumbs to top pudding or ice cream. Cut each loaf into 9 slices and evenly space, cut side–down, on an ungreased baking sheet. Return to oven and bake for 10 minutes. Turn slices; bake 10 minutes longer or until crisp and golden brown. Remove to wire racks; turn off oven.

4. Place wire racks with rusks in cooled oven and leave overnight. Store in an airtight container; a tin is best.

DAILY BREADS AND ROLLS

LAZY-DAY SUMMER WHOLE WHEAT BREAD

[makes 2 loaves]

Many farms across the Range, especially those owned by Scandinavian immigrants, had outbuildings—often as an adjunct to a sauna—complete with wood cookstoves that functioned as summer kitchens so the cooking, canning, and baking could take place without heating the house. This bread arose from the summertime needs of homemakers in towns, where the houses were close together with no fans to cool the small kitchens with their wood-heated stoves, when air conditioning had yet to be imagined.

* * *

Vigorously stirring the yeast into the warm water, using soured milk or butter-milk for part or all of the liquid, and adding baking powder to the flour not only improves the leavening; it eliminates the need for double-proofing while still producing a good loaf. There's less cleanup because the dough is kneaded only once before being placed into loaf pans for a single rising, and the operation becomes even more efficient with quick-rise yeast and bread flour, which is high in gluten.* Powdered buttermilk is another great convenience product that eliminates the need to buy whole quarts when only a few cups are needed. It keeps indefinitely and has multiple uses. Rolling the dough before shaping it into loaves further helps the gluten development. Because this is a sticky dough, a baker's bench knife is a good tool to have; it will serve you well elsewhere in the kitchen.

*Bread (high-gluten) flour has a high protein content, which is necessary for gluten development, the property that allows bread to rise and gives it structure.

¾ cup warm water (105–115 degrees)

2 packets (4 teaspoons) quick-rise yeast

2 tablespoons brown sugar or molasses

2 teaspoons kosher or sea salt

2 cups bread flour, divided

1¼ cups buttermilk, fresh or reconstituted, at room temperature or slightly warmed

¼ cup shortening

3 cups whole or cracked wheat flour

2 tablespoons butter, melted

1. Have all ingredients at room temperature or warmer before beginning. Place the warm water in a large bowl, sprinkle on the yeast, and stir vigorously with a fork for a minute to dissolve the yeast and speed up the action; let stand for a minute or two. Add brown sugar or molasses, salt, and ¼ cup bread flour, stirring vigorously. Let rest for another 2 minutes.

2. Stir in buttermilk, 1 cup bread flour, and shortening. Use an electric mixer on low speed to blend until ingredients are smooth, with the shortening well integrated. Add whole wheat flour 1 cup at a time, using mixer until it becomes too thick. Stir in ¼ cup bread flour by hand followed by remaining wheat flour until all the liquid is absorbed. The dough should be soft and slightly sticky; add more bread flour if needed.

3. Sprinkle some of the remaining ½ cup bread flour over cutting board or work surface; turn out dough and begin to knead, using a metal spatula to scrape up

>>

dough that sticks and dusting with remaining bread flour as necessary. Knead for 7 to 8 minutes (4 to 5 minutes if using a stand mixer and a dough hook). Divide in two, set aside, covered with mixing bowl, and let rest for 5 minutes. While dough is resting, brush 2 standard (9 x 5–inch) loaf pans with some of the melted butter; reserve remainder for tops of loaves.

4. Scrape work surface and dust with flour. Roll each portion of dough into a rectangle, the short side equal to the length of the loaf pan. Roll up dough like a jelly roll; pinch seam and ends; place in prepared pan seam side–down and tuck ends under. Brush with remaining butter, cover with waxed paper or plastic wrap, and set in a warm place (80–85 degrees) or a warming drawer set on low until the dough has risen 1 inch above the sides of the pan, 45 to 50 minutes. While dough is rising, preheat oven to 425 degrees.

5. Bake 30 to 35 minutes, until loaves are golden brown on top and loose in the pans. If they are browning too fast (especially in a convection oven), cover with aluminum foil or brown parchment paper. Turn out of pan and thump on bottom to test for doneness; they should sound hollow. Place on wire rack and cool before serving.

RUISNÄKKILEIPÄ / FINNISH HARDTACK

[makes 4 (12-inch) rounds]

The signature center hole found in rounds of real Scandinavian hardtack is a truly functional decoration. This rye flour–based cracker was a dietary mainstay that saw families through the long, dark winters, when it filled in for a lack of crisp, fresh vegetables. In the fall, large batches would be baked with a center hole in each round big enough to thread a long broom handle or thin tree branch through. These would be hung from a ceiling in a dark location, often the root cellar, where they dried and were kept through the winter.

As the base for pickled and smoked fish, cheeses, cured meats, and pâtés eaten at morning breakfasts, midday coffee times, and late-evening lunches, hardtack is always present on Scandinavian family tables: in Norway as *knaakkebrod*; in Sweden as *knäckebröd*; and in Finland, where the custom of pole-drying is thought to have originated, as *Ruisnäkkileipä*. The recipe is simple, with only four ingredients, one rising, and no kneading, and is just as delicious when oven dried instead of in the traditional pole manner. Either version tastes equally good with a smear of just plain butter as a side to Thursday Pea Soup with Ginger, Orange, and Smoked Ham (page 120).

2 cups warm water (105–115 degrees)	1 teaspoon kosher or sea salt
2 tablespoons regular dry yeast	4–5 cups coarse-grained rye flour

1. Fill a large glass or ceramic bowl with hot water or place in a low oven to warm for a few minutes. Drain bowl and add measured warm water; stir in yeast until dissolved, followed by salt. Beat flour in gradually—about 4 cups—until a soft dough forms. Cover the bowl with a dish towel and set in a warm place to rise until doubled, about an hour. Preheat oven to 450 degrees. Grease and flour 4 unrimmed baking sheets (see notes).

2. Lightly sprinkle a countertop or work surface with some of the remaining flour, turn dough onto countertop, and divide and shape into 4 balls. Carefully roll out each ball into a 12-inch circle about ¼ to ½ inch thick, dusting with just enough flour to keep the dough from sticking to the rolling pin and the counter. Try not to work in too much of the extra cup of flour. Slide one or two long metal spatulas under the dough and carefully transfer rounds to the prepared baking sheets. Prick the surface of each round with the tines of a fork, and use a small (2-inch) cookie cutter or jar lid to cut a hole in the centers; this will help the moisture escape during baking. Let rise, uncovered, in a warm place for 15 minutes.

3. Bake for 10 to 15 minutes, until the breads feel very firm but not hard. Remove from oven to a cooling rack; turn off oven. Place cooling rack with the crackers into the cooled oven and let dry 6 to 8 hours or overnight, with the door slightly open. Break into large pieces for serving. Store in tightly covered tins.

Cook's Notes: *Rye flour is heavy, with only a trace of gluten. Warming a large glass or ceramic bowl with hot water or in a low oven before starting will help leaven the dough. If your baking sheets have sides, flip them over and bake the dough on the bottoms; all the moisture must bake out for the cracker to dry properly.*

Rye Bread

Rye is the flour most commonly associated with the breads of the Germanic, Scandinavian, and Slavic countries. Flavors and textures vary from the floral orange-anise notes found in Swedish breads to the earthy loaves of German and sour Polish caraway ryes. Frugal housewives often saved the water from boiling potatoes to use the next day in bread and soup. The sugars in the starchy water give the yeast an extra boost, which helps "make good rise" in these hearty, dense breads. Another tip for a good rise is to make a sponge. Sprinkle a few tablespoons of high-gluten bread flour over the warm potato water and yeast—don't stir in—and set in a warm, draft-free location until the mixture bubbles and the surface resembles the side of a sponge. The sponge method works for breads made from white flour as well.

SWEDISH *LIMPA* / RYE BREAD

[makes 2 large loaves]

Most cultures have a version of rye bread, each with its own characteristics, often reflected in the name. In Swedish rye bread is *limpa*, in reference to the inclusion of a sweetener—usually molasses or honey—and citrus, as well as some sweeter, licorice-flavored spices like fennel, anise, or cardamom.

• • •

This traditional round rye loaf is a two-day undertaking—well worth the time—and a great winter weekend project to do with the kids. Start on Saturday night, then bake and serve fresh from the oven on Sunday, with a generous smear of salted butter and some homemade currant or highbush cranberry jelly.

½ cup molasses	1 tablespoon fennel seed
2½ cups water	¼ cup shortening
⅔ cup firmly packed dark brown sugar	3 packets (2 tablespoons) quick-rise yeast
2 teaspoons salt	

½ cup warm water
(105–115 degrees)

3 tablespoons bread flour

4 cups medium rye flour, sifted

5 cups bread flour, sifted, plus
½ cup for kneading

about 2 tablespoons salted
butter, melted

1. In a saucepan, mix together molasses, 2½ cups water, brown sugar, and salt. Grind fennel and add to the saucepan. Bring mixture to the boiling point over high heat. Lower heat and simmer uncovered for 5 minutes. Remove from heat, stir in shortening, and let stand until lukewarm.

2. In a large mixing bowl, dissolve yeast in the ½ cup warm water; sprinkle the 3 tablespoons bread flour over the top, cover with plastic, and set aside in a warm place for 15 minutes for sponge to form. Add cooled molasses mixture to the sponge and mix well. Stir in the rye flour. Beat with a stainless or bread spoon* until smooth. Cover with plastic wrap and a clean dish towel; let rise overnight at room temperature in a draft-free location, about 9 to 10 hours.

3. In the morning sift 4 cups of the bread flour over the rye-yeast sponge and mix in by hand; work in as much of the remaining cup of flour as the mixture will take without becoming too stiff. Sprinkle the ½ cup of flour on a pastry cloth or work surface for kneading. Turn the dough out onto the floured surface and knead until smooth and elastic, 8 to 10 minutes. Place in a greased bowl, rotating the dough so the entire surface is coated; cover with plastic wrap and let rise until doubled, 2 to 2½ hours.

4. Cut dough in half; shape into 2 round loaves and place in 2 greased 9-inch pie pans (don't use glass). Prick the tops all over with the tines of a dinner fork, cover with a clean cloth, and place in a warm, draft-free spot; let rise until light, about 1 hour.

5. Preheat oven to 350 degrees. Bake for 45 to 55 minutes, until loaves sound hollow when you tap the bottoms. Remove from pie pans to a wire cooling rack and brush tops with melted butter.

*A bread spoon is a wooden spoon that has an open loop in place of the bowl; a very old-fashioned cooking implement that is still available in specialty kitchen stores.

ANNA SOPHIA'S *SÖT SUR BRÖD* / SWEDISH SWEET-SOUR CARAWAY RYE BREAD

[makes 2 large or 4 small loaves]

My great-grandmother Johanna Vörgren taught her daughter, my great-aunt Anna Sophia Eliason, how to make this bread in southern Finland during the early days of the twentieth century. Anna Sophia brought the recipe with her when she immigrated to America in 1912, and she taught it to her young daughter, (Anna) Linnea, in the 1920s. Linnea passed the tradition of how to bake it in a wood-fired kitchen range—and the story of how her mother learned to make it—on to me in the 1960s, when I was a teenager.

. . .

This bread was originally made with cake yeast and all-purpose white flour. I've updated the ingredients to reflect the times. If using high-gluten bread flour, including baking soda to help leaven the heavier rye and whole wheat flours is optional.

3 packets (2 tablespoons) quick-rise yeast, or 2 tablespoons plus ¾ teaspoon quick-rise yeast granules

½ cup warm water

1 teaspoon white sugar

2 tablespoons bread flour

2 cups water

¼ cup vegetable oil

⅓ cup white sugar

⅓ cup brown sugar

½ cup molasses

2 tablespoons kosher or sea salt

1 teaspoon each of anise, caraway, and fennel seeds

4 cups buttermilk

1 teaspoon baking soda, optional (see head note)

5 cups rye flour

5 cups white bread flour (substitute 1 cup whole wheat flour if desired)

½ cup brown coffee syrup (recipe follows)

1. To make the starter sponge, dissolve yeast in ½ cup warm water with the teaspoon of white sugar. Sprinkle the 2 tablespoons of bread flour over the top; cover with plastic wrap and set aside in a warm spot until top is covered with foam, 20 to 30 minutes. While the sponge is proofing, put 2 cups water, oil, ⅓ cup white sugar, brown sugar, molasses, salt, and seeds in a saucepan; stir and bring to a boil;

cool slightly. Place the buttermilk in a large bowl; stir in baking soda (if using). Add the hot water–molasses mixture, followed by the rye flour; stir until completely absorbed, then add the yeast mixture. Mix in white flour (including whole wheat flour, if using) in three or four increments and knead in the bowl to form a shaggy mass of dough. Turn out onto a floured cloth or surface and continue kneading until flour is just absorbed, 8 to 10 minutes. Depending on the level of humidity the dough may not take all the flour or if too sticky may need a bit more.

2. Wash and dry the mixing bowl and grease with shortening. Shape the dough into a large round and put in greased mixing bowl, turning to coat entire surface. Cover with a dish towel and put in a warm place until doubled, about 1 hour. When ready, turn dough out onto the floured surface, punch down, cover with the mixing bowl, and let rest for 10 to 15 minutes. Divide the dough with a sharp knife, and shape into 2 large or 4 small round loaves. Place into greased pie pans (do not use glass), cover with towel, and let rise until doubled, about 45 minutes.

3. Preheat oven to 350 degrees. Make the hot syrup. Prick the tops of the loaves with the tines of a dinner fork. Brush with one-third of the coffee syrup; this forms a sweet, slightly sticky crust. Bake for 30 minutes, remove from oven, brush with half the remaining syrup, and return to oven for another 30 minutes. Remove a loaf from its pan to test for doneness: the bottom should be brown and firm. Once out of the oven, brush warm loaves with remaining syrup while still in the pie pans. Remove from pans to a cooling rack. Let cool at least 20 minutes before slicing.

Cook's Notes: *This bread is delicious served open faced, topped with salted butter, marmalade, cranberry or currant jelly, and thinly sliced hard cheeses, ham, or salami.*

BROWN COFFEE SYRUP

A good use for leftover morning coffee. If you have enough, bring it to a boil and reduce for really strong coffee flavor.

¼ cup strong black coffee ¼ cup water

3 tablespoons white sugar

Heat coffee to a simmer; add sugar and water. Bring to a boil, stirring to dissolve sugar. Boil for 3 to 4 minutes. Remove from heat; set aside, and keep warm for brushing on loaves.

The Joy of Making Bread

[by Anna Linnea Eliason]

Linnea Eliason feeding her chickens on her farm outside Hibbing, 2012

Written *on the back of the recipe she gave me the day she taught me how to make her mother's* Söt Sur Bröd, *on her family farm outside Hibbing, Minnesota, June 1968.*

My mother instilled in me the joy of making bread. The knowledge of good flour, how it is grown and milled. The importance it has in our daily living. She would mix the ingredients when we all got old enough to knead it for her. We always had homemade bread and biscuit. In winter we would make a batch of Sweet Sour Bread when the kitchen range was going full swing. Is there any better aroma than bread baking when you come in from the outside?

She told me stories how they made bread in Finland when she was growing up. They had a long trough-like bench, and made many loaves at one time. She was in her early teens working for some farmers where an elderly man who was considered odd sat and watched her kneading it, which was a heavy job. He thumped his hand and spoke out loud, "Can't you at least get the flour for her!"

"In the Lord's Prayer—'Give us this day our daily bread.' *Both spiritual and physical!*"

ITALIAN DAILY BREAD AND ROLLS

[makes 1 large or 2 small loaves or 12 rolls]

Pane importante versatile! Italians take their bread seriously. This very plain, versatile dough is given multiple forms and functions in the Italian culinary catalog. It appears—freshly baked—at all meals on the daily table as long, round, or square crusty loaves of bread or rolls, chewy breadsticks, or skinnier, crispier crostini. And when rolled into thin circles or rectangles, it serves as the base for that internationally important Neapolitan offering: pizza. Day-old loaves are sliced and toasted for *bruschetta,* used as the base for panzanella (page 115), or dried and crushed for thickening soups, sauces, pastas, and ragouts. Also great unbuttered with a pear and a glass of dry red Italian wine, and a *must* for porketta sandwiches (page 68).

. . .

A crusty exterior and a soft, airy interior are the two defining characteristics of a good Italian bread, and the two critical keys to achieving such a loaf are time

and temperature. In this recipe the ingredients are few: only four excluding water. In comparison to most bread recipes, the small amounts combined with yeast in cold water might make leavening seem doubtful, but the long fermentation lets the yeast multiply while the dough is resting, in both warm and cold environments. This in turn produces the flavor and texture unique to this bread. The rolls freeze well; to reheat, place frozen rolls in a brown paper bag, spritz bag with water, and place in a low, preheated oven, 150 to 200 degrees, for ten minutes.

STARTER

½ cup cool water, filtered if possible

⅛ teaspoon quick-rise yeast

1 cup all-purpose flour

DOUGH

1 cup warm water
(105–115 degrees)

¼ teaspoon quick-rise yeast

1½ teaspoons sea salt

3½ cups all-purpose flour

EGG WASH

1 large egg white mixed with 1–2 tablespoons cool water

1. To make the starter, in a narrow, medium, stainless steel bowl (see notes), combine cool water and ⅛ teaspoon yeast; add flour slowly, stirring until smooth. Cover tightly with plastic wrap, and refrigerate overnight.

2. The next day, remove starter from the refrigerator and transfer to a large bowl; add 1 cup warm water, ¼ teaspoon yeast, and salt, stirring to blend. Add flour 1 cup at a time, stirring with a wooden spoon until dough becomes stiff; mix in remaining flour by hand, scraping dough from sides of the bowl. Continue working in remaining flour, and begin kneading in the bowl until a soft, cohesive dough forms, 5 to 6 minutes; it may be a bit sticky and rough.

3. Cover bowl with plastic wrap, and set in a warm place away from drafts to rise for 1 hour. Punch down dough and turn over in the bowl; re-cover with plastic and let rise for another 2 hours. Turn dough out onto a lightly *greased* work surface, cover with bowl, and let rest for 10 to 15 minutes. Remove bowl, knead briefly, 1 to 2 minutes, and shape into a large oval loaf, or divide into 12 pieces with a sharp knife and shape by rolling under your cupped hands until firm balls are formed. Line an unrimmed baking sheet with parchment and place bread or rolls, evenly spaced, onto the pan; loosely cover with a clean dish

towel, and set aside to rise until puffed but not doubled, 1 to 2 hours. The rolls will have flattened slightly but will recover when baked. Place in refrigerator, covered, for 2 to 3 hours.

4. Half an hour before removing dough from refrigerator, preheat oven to 425 degrees. Whisk egg white and water until frothy. Brush bread or rolls, and make 3 diagonal slashes, ¼ inch deep, along the top of the loaf with a very sharp knife or razor blade or a single slash on each roll. Put in oven and immediately reduce the temperature to 375 degrees. Bake bread for 25 to 30 minutes; bake rolls for 20 to 25 minutes, until golden brown. Remove from oven to a cooling rack; or for a better crust, turn off oven, open door, and allow rolls to cool in place.

Cook's Notes: *Proofing the starter in a tall, narrow bowl or cylinder will increase its volume by keeping the gases contained; stainless steel is best. This recipe responds well to mixing with a dough hook attachment in a stand mixer. It works well in a bread machine when all ingredients, including the prepared starter, which has rested overnight in the refrigerator, are combined at the same time.*

MILK BREAD

[makes 2 loaves]

Milk bread is white bread personified: light with an airy texture and—except for the yeast and water—all the ingredients are white. This bread was universally embraced by mid-thirties America as the refined counterpart to the thick, coarse-grained loaves made in most immigrant homes. White bread's popularity took hold in the 1950s with the soft, gummy commercial versions baby boomers considered "wonderful," but those all pale in comparison to this loaf.

• • •

The light, creamy texture is a result of sifting the flour and employing a straight batter method in the making. Its sweet flavor turns slightly tangy when buttermilk is used in part or in place of the whole milk. Milk bread freezes well and is great for toast and tea sandwiches. Try it for a classic PB&J or toasted BLT.

1 cup whole milk or buttermilk

1 cup water

½ cup shortening, plus more for bowl and pans

5½ cups all-purpose flour, sifted, divided

¼ teaspoon baking soda

2½ teaspoons fine salt

3½ tablespoons white sugar

1 packet (2 teaspoons) quick-rise yeast

1. Combine milk or buttermilk, water, and ½ cup shortening in a small pan and heat until warm; the shortening need not totally melt. The buttermilk may cause the mixture to curdle, but it doesn't matter.

2. While the liquid is heating, re-sift flour with baking soda and salt into a large bowl; stir sugar and yeast together in a small bowl, and add to flour mixture. Gradually add warm liquid to the dry ingredients; beat for 2 minutes on medium with a hand mixer, scraping bowl once or twice.

3. Turn onto a lightly floured surface, cover with the mixing bowl, and let rest for 5 minutes. Gently knead until smooth and elastic, about 8 minutes. If dough seems too soft or sticky, add a small amount of additional flour.

4. Wash and dry the bowl; grease with shortening. Place kneaded ball of dough in the bowl, turning to coat. Cover with plastic wrap, set in a warm place (80–85 degrees), and let rise until doubled in bulk, about 1 hour; or put in a warming drawer on the lowest setting and let rise 45 to 50 minutes. Grease 2 (8½ x 4½-inch) loaf pans. Punch down dough, cut in half, and gently shape each into an oblong slightly smaller than the length of the pan. Place in pans, cover with plastic wrap or waxed paper, and return to warm place for 45 minutes or until dough has risen 1 inch above the pans. Preheat oven to 375 degrees (350 if using a glass pan).

5. Bake for about 40 minutes, until golden brown and bottom of loaf sounds hollow when thumped. If bottom is still soft, return to the oven without the pan for an additional 5 to 10 minutes; an inserted wooden pick or metal skewer should come out clean and dry. Cool loaves on a wire rack.

POTATO ROLLS

[makes 24 rolls or 2 loaves]

Potatoes were one of the more important, economical, and readily available staples for the immigrants. One seed potato generated four or five, which in turn produced twenty more, which resulted in bushels—enough to sustain large families through long winters and economic hardships. The ways to prepare them seem endless, and they can be eaten in their entirety, with leftovers finding their way into breads and cakes, soups and sauces. The wise housewife used every bit, right down to the starch-rich cooking water and, in the case of the Scandinavians, in the beloved spirit of the Baltic: aquavit.

• • •

Potato water is one of the more important ingredients in these rolls; the starch released by the peeled, boiled potatoes is critical to the texture and taste. This recipe makes two dozen rolls or two generous loaves or a combination. Both freeze well. These are great for sandwiches with egg salad, with soups and stews, or as an absorbent late-night lunch side after multiple shots of aquavit. Skoal!

2 medium russet or red potatoes, peeled

¼ cup warm water (105–115 degrees)

1 packet (2 teaspoons) quick-rise yeast

2 tablespoons white sugar

2 tablespoons all-purpose flour

8 tablespoons (1 stick) salted butter, at room temperature, divided

1 tablespoon kosher or sea salt

5–6 cups bread flour, plus more for dusting

flaked sea salt, optional

1. Boil the potatoes in 2 cups of unsalted water. Once cooked, remove potatoes. Reserve 1½ cups of the cooking water; mash or rice potatoes and reserve 1 cup. Set both aside.

2. Place ¼ cup warm water in a small bowl, sprinkle on the yeast, and stir in sugar; sprinkle all-purpose flour over top, cover with plastic wrap, and set aside in a warm place (80–85 degrees) for 15 minutes, until yeast begins to bubble.

3. Place 4 tablespoons softened butter in a large bowl. Reheat reserved potato water with 1 tablespoon salt to 120 degrees. Pour over butter, and stir until but-

>>

ter has melted; stir in activated yeast mixture. Add ¾ cup reserved potatoes and stir until combined; mixture should be loose but not runny; add remaining potatoes to thicken if needed. Add bread flour to liquid mixture 1 cup at a time, stirring with a wooden spoon. Continue adding flour until a stiff dough begins to form; work in additional flour by hand until dough pulls cleanly away from the sides of the bowl in a rough mass.

4. Dust a work surface with flour, turn out dough, and knead vigorously until smooth and elastic, 8 to 10 minutes, adding more flour to the work surface if dough is sticky. Form into a ball, rub with some of the remaining butter, and return to the bowl; cover with plastic wrap and set aside in a warm place (80–85 degrees) until more than doubled in bulk, about 1½ hours; dough is ready when holes made by poking fingers into the surface remain.

5. Remove plastic, punch down dough, and turn out onto floured surface; knead for 30 seconds to 1 minute to remove air bubbles. Cut into 2 pieces, cover with a dish towel, and let rest for 1 minute for rolls; 10 minutes for loaves. *For rolls*: roll each piece into a cylinder about 18 inches long; cut each cylinder into 12 equal pieces. Shape into balls by rolling under cupped hands. Place on greased baking sheets, spacing evenly, cover with towels and let rise in a warm place until doubled in size, 15 to 20 minutes. *For loaves*, flatten each piece into a 4 x 6–inch rectangle; fold in half, pinch long edge together. Place in buttered loaf pan, seam side–down. Cover with a towel and let rise in a warm place until double in size, 30 to 35 minutes.

6. Preheat oven to 400 degrees. Uncover rolls/loaves, lightly brush or spritz tops with water, sprinkle with flaked sea salt (if using), and lightly dust tops with flour. *For rolls:* place in oven, reduce heat to 350 degrees, and bake until tops and bottoms are lightly browned, 15 to 20 minutes. *For loaves:* bake 15 minutes; reduce heat to 350 degrees. Continue baking until loaves pull away from sides of pan and bottom crusts lift away from pan and tops are lightly browned, no longer than 30 to 35 minutes. Remove to wire racks; brush tops with any remaining butter, cool slightly, and serve, or let cool to room temperature before storing in sealed plastic bags.

Cook's Notes: *These rolls, with their wonderful, creamy texture, freeze well. Tightly wrap in aluminum foil, then place in zip-top bags.*

ISOÄITI'S PULLA / FINNISH BISCUIT (GRANDMOTHER'S CARDAMOM BREAD)

[makes 2 loaves]

This fragrant, buttery, sweet Finnish coffee bread is always referred to as "biscuit," though it's nothing like a shortbread or scone. With the inclusion of eggs, it's more like a brioche in composition, but fluffier and more delicate in texture. Everyone's recipe seems to call for exactly ten cardamom seeds, and many crush them using the same "traditional method" recorded by Grandma Suomu in 1965: "Wrap up the seeds tight in a dish towel that you made from an empty flour or grain sack that you washed with bleach and hung outside to dry in the sun. Then you press down on the towel with your littlest cast-iron skillet, and rub it back and forth a time or two; or you could use your rolling pin, but the pan works real good."

• • •

The traditional shape for *pulla* is a braid baked in a loaf pan with the ends tucked under, though some prefer baking it full length on a baking sheet; it can also be made into small knotted rolls. Try it lightly toasted with a dab of sweet, unsalted butter, or briefly dip slices in an egg wash, fry until golden, and serve with Lingonberry Sauce (page 53) for some Baltic-style French toast.

SPONGE

⅓ cup warm water or whole milk
(105–115 degrees)

1 packet (2 teaspoons) quick-
rise yeast

2 teaspoons white sugar

1 tablespoon bread flour

LOAF

2 cups whole milk, heated
almost to boiling

⅔ cup white sugar

½ teaspoon sea or kosher salt

10 cardamom seeds, crushed
(see head note)

>>

| ⅓ cup (5⅓ tablespoons) unsalted butter | 2 large eggs, beaten |
| | 7 cups bread flour |

1. To make the sponge: Put warmed ⅓ cup water or milk in a medium glass bowl, add yeast, and stir to dissolve. Sprinkle 2 teaspoons sugar over the yeast followed by 1 tablespoon flour; don't stir. Cover with plastic wrap and set in a warm place for 20 to 30 minutes or until bubbling. While sponge is working, heat the 2 cups milk and add ⅔ cup sugar, salt, cardamom, and butter, stirring to dissolve; set aside to cool.

2. To make the dough: When sponge is ready, transfer to a large bowl and add lukewarm milk mixture and beaten eggs; stir to combine. Slowly stir in sifted flour 1 cup at a time, vigorously beating the batter after each addition until dough becomes too stiff to stir. Turn out onto a lightly floured surface and knead until it is soft and light, 10 to 12 minutes, adding just enough flour to prevent sticking. Form into a ball and place in a lightly buttered bowl, turning dough to coat. Cover with plastic wrap and place in a warm spot to rise until doubled, about 1½ hours. Punch down dough, turn out of bowl onto a lightly floured surface, cover with bowl, and let rest for 10 to 15 minutes.

Lefse Logistics

It's not difficult to make the Norwegian equivalent of the French crêpe or Mexican flour tortilla, but it does take time, practice, and investment in a few specialized pieces of equipment to master and make in the true and proper *Norske* fashion. Lefse rolling pins, lefse turning sticks, lefse griddles, lefse rolling cloths, even lefse lids and cozies—it all elicits an *Uff da!*

Since these inexpensive, oversized pancakes seem to be ubiquitous in Minnesota, especially during the high holiday season in December, rather than a recipe of this traditional bread, I've opted to offer a brief history, which underscores the effort involved.

3. To shape the loaves: Remove bowl and cut dough in two, setting one portion back in the bowl. Divide first half into 3 equal pieces; roll with lightly buttered hands until each is 12 inches long. Lay pieces next to each other, pinch all three together at one end, and braid. Repeat with the second portion of dough. If making loaves, butter 2 standard (8½ x 4½–inch) loaf pans, fold ends of braids under, and tuck into the pans. For flat braids, line 2 baking sheets with parchment, lightly brush melted butter over area dough will cover, and place braids on pans. Cover breads with a dish towel and set in a warm place to rise, 35 to 40 minutes.

4. Preheat oven to 375 degrees. Bake for 25 to 30 minutes, until golden brown. The shaped loaves will take a bit longer than the flat braids.

Cook's Notes: *Coarse-grained baker's sanding sugar sprinkled over the tops adds an attractive, textured finish to the loaves. Sanding sugar can be found in most specialty cooking stores or online baking shops. Mix ½ cup white sugar with 2 tablespoons warm water; brush tops while bread is still warm, and lightly sprinkle with grains of sanding sugar.*

The Lefse Tradition

[by Bob Brooke, courtesy AllScandinavia.com]

Lefse is to any Norwegian what a tortilla is to any Mexican—a staple of life. It was something grandmothers made for their families during the holidays.

In Norway women would travel from house to house spending three or four days baking [up] to a year's supply of *lefse* for the household, working over an open fire and by lantern light into the evening. When they finished, they stacked the rounds in barrels. They also stored the rounds in *kistes* or sea chests or in steamer trunks for fishermen who were packing provisions for long sea voyages. To wash down the lefse, people often brewed homemade beer in the same shed.

JULEKAKA / NORWEGIAN CHRISTMAS BRAID

[makes 2 large or 4 small loaves]

This overnight method for the Norwegian holiday bread is actually a timesaver. All the ingredients—except for the fruit—are directly combined and set aside to rise overnight, or all day while you are away at work. This recipe calls for active dry yeast rather than the quick-rise type. Because the first rising is twelve hours or overnight in a warm environment, quick-rise yeast might play out in the second rising. The use of active dry yeast ensures the rise won't be impeded after the incorporation of the heavy dried fruits.

The traditional citron and raisins have been replaced by dried apricots and cranberries for a bit of an update. Make one large loaf for your family and two small loaves to give as gifts.

2 cups whole milk

1 cup white sugar

1½ teaspoons kosher or sea salt

8 tablespoons (1 stick) unsalted butter, at room temperature, plus 2 tablespoons for greasing bowl

7 cups bread flour

¾ teaspoon ground cardamom

2 packets (4 teaspoons) active dry yeast (see head note)

¾ cup finely chopped dried apricots

¾ cup dried cranberries

1 large egg yolk beaten with 2 tablespoons half-and-half or whole milk

Confectioners' Sugar Glaze (recipe follows), optional

1. Place milk in a medium saucepan with sugar, salt, and 8 tablespoons of butter; heat just long enough for butter to melt. Grease a large bowl with 2 tablespoons of butter. Remove mixture from heat and let cool before pouring into the buttered bowl. While milk is cooling, place flour, cardamom, and yeast in a separate bowl, stirring to combine. Add flour mixture to the cooled milk mixture 1 cup at a time, mixing well after each addition. Cover with a clean dish towel and set in a warm place—80 to 85 degrees—to rise for 12 hours or overnight.

2. In the morning, punch down dough, turn out onto a floured surface, and pat out into a 12-inch circle. Dust apricots and cranberries with a little flour, sprinkle

over the dough, and knead until the dough is satiny smooth and the fruit is evenly distributed, 10 to 12 minutes. Divide and form into round loaves, 2 large or 4 small; place on lightly greased baking sheets, cover with a towel, and set in a warm place until doubled in bulk, about 1 hour.

3. Preheat oven to 350 degrees. Brush tops of loaves with egg wash and bake for 45 minutes for large loaves or 35 minutes for small. Remove to cooling rack. Brush tops with some melted butter while still warm, or glaze with thin confectioners' sugar icing when cool.

BASIC CONFECTIONERS' SUGAR GLAZE

Mix 1 cup sifted confectioners' sugar with 1–2 tablespoons of whole milk until smooth; reduce or increase milk for desired thickness to use as a frosting or a glaze. Flavorings such as vanilla, almond, or orange extract or ground cardamom, ginger, or cinnamon may also be added to taste.

POTICA

[makes 3 loaves]

"When I asked the children how many eat *potica*, every hand went up," said Mr. Scott, Ironworld Discovery Center director, recalling a visit to a sociology class at Hibbing High School. "When I asked how many of their mothers made *potica*, a handful of hands went up. When I asked how many [of their] grandmothers make it, all the hands went up." Thus, one of Ironworld's goals, he said, is to preserve the culinary traditions of the grandmothers' generation.

. . .

Potica (pronounced *po-TEE-zah*) might just be the best example of a cross-cultural culinary exchange. Rare is the Iron Range wedding, funeral, or holiday buffet that doesn't include this sweet Slovenian bread. *Potica* experts—and there are many—recommend pulling the dough out on a table that you can access from all sides, especially if you have people to help with the stretching. Having two or even four sets of hands makes this step go faster while lessening the chance of tearing, and usually results in an even, thin sheet of dough. The professional *potica* makers say it must be "thin enough to read the newspaper through."

DOUGH

¼ cup warm water (105–110 degrees)

1 packet (2 teaspoons) quick-rise yeast

¼ cup white sugar, divided

¾ cup whole milk, heated almost to boiling, then cooled slightly

½ teaspoon vanilla

dash salt

1 medium egg, lightly beaten

3–3½ cups bread flour or unbleached all-purpose flour

4 tablespoons (½ stick) salted butter, melted

FILLING

⅓ cup heavy cream

1¼ pounds walnuts, finely ground

4 tablespoons (½ stick) salted butter, melted

¾ cup white sugar

1 cup brown sugar

¼ cup light honey

2 large eggs plus 1 large egg yolk

1. Place warm water in a large bowl and sprinkle in the yeast along with 1 teaspoon of the sugar; stir to dissolve. In a separate bowl, combine the milk, vanilla, salt, egg, and remaining sugar; whisk together and add to the yeast, stirring to combine. Stir in the flour 1 cup at a time until dough gets too stiff; then add 4 tablespoons melted butter and work in by hand. Add remaining flour, and knead until the mixture forms a smooth ball, 8 to 10 minutes. Place in a large greased bowl, cover, and let rise in a warm place for about 1½ hours. Do not punch down.

2. Reserve 1 tablespoon cream. Combine the ground walnuts, 4 tablespoons melted butter, both sugars, honey, and 2 whole eggs, mixing well. Gradually beat in remaining cream until the mixture is the consistency of spun honey.

3. On a table or other flat surface that is at least 4 x 6 feet, spread a clean sheet so that the edges hang slightly over the sides; lightly flour the surface. Roll out the dough to form a 9 x 13–inch rectangle. Place your hands under the dough palms up. Lift the dough up several inches and begin pulling it toward you with your fingertips. Carefully stretch it out, trying not to tear the dough, lifting and pulling until it is evenly thin and transparent, about 3 x 5 feet.

4. Preheat oven to 325 degrees and position rack in the middle. Spread the filling evenly over the surface of the dough, leaving a ¾-inch margin around all the sides. Starting at one of the narrower sides, fold the unfilled edge of dough over an inch of the filling. Reach across the table to lift the edge of the sheet up and over, and down close to the filling. Pull slowly toward you, rolling the dough over the filling as you go, keeping the sheet low to ensure a tight jelly roll–style dough wrapped around the filling.

5. Cut roll into thirds. Grease a 9 x 13–inch baking dish and line with aluminum foil, shiny side up; lightly butter the entire foil surface, including the sides. Place the three *poticas* on the foil, seam side–down and evenly spaced, with additional strips of buttered foil between them. Mix the egg yolk with the remaining tablespoon of cream, and brush over the tops and sides. Bake for 45 minutes to 1 hour or until golden brown.

Cook's Notes: *A word of caution: don't bake this bread on a convection setting if your oven has one; it will dry the outer crust too much. Serve with thinly sliced ham or prosciutto and some salted butter, or thin slices of a salty hard white cheese. And coffee—of course.*

CHALLAH

[makes 2 loaves]

Challah is the braided egg bread found on Judaic Sabbath tables for more than several millennia. Early Jewish settlers brought this religious food custom to the Iron Range, where they keep it still. Traditionally eaten torn, not sliced, this bread boasts a rich, dense crumb that lends itself very well to being transformed into French toast.

• • •

Following Hebrew dictate and tradition, this recipe is dairy free and takes its sweetness from honey rather than sugar. A pinch of saffron has been included to bring added brightness to the loaf.

SPONGE

1 packet (2 teaspoons) quick-rise yeast

½ cup warm water (105–115 degrees)

2 tablespoons light-colored honey

¼ cup bread flour

DOUGH

2 large eggs and 1 large egg white,* at room temperature

6 tablespoons canola or vegetable oil

*Save yolk for glaze.

pinch saffron

1½ teaspoons kosher salt

¾ cup warm water (115–120 degrees)

4½ cups bread flour, divided

GLAZE

1 large egg yolk, beaten

1 tablespoon cold water

1 tablespoon light-colored honey

1 teaspoon sesame or poppy seeds, optional

1. To make the sponge, in a small bowl, stir yeast into warm water until dissolved; stir in honey and sprinkle ¼ cup flour over the top. Cover with plastic wrap and set in a warm place (80–85 degrees) until foamy, about 15 minutes. While sponge is working, in a large bowl, beat eggs and egg white together with the oil. In a small bowl or mixing cup, stir saffron and salt into the warm water until dissolved; stir into egg-oil mixture.

2. When the sponge is ready, stir into egg mixture. Stir 2 cups of flour into liquid ingredients, 1 cup at a time, mixing well after each addition. Beat for 3 minutes by hand (2 minutes with an electric mixer), until thick batter forms. Stir in remaining flour with a wooden spoon until no longer sticky; if too wet, add small amounts of flour until dough cleans the inside of the bowl. Turn out onto a floured surface and knead until the dough is smooth and elastic, 8 to 10 minutes. Wipe bowl clean, grease with oil, and add dough, turning to coat. Cover tightly with plastic wrap; set in a warm place (80–85 degrees) until doubled, about 1 hour.

3. Punch down dough, kneading out air bubbles; turn out onto floured surface and divide in half. Divide each half into 3 equal pieces; roll each into a 12-inch length. Lay 3 pieces parallel to each other, pinch together at the top, and braid, starting with the middle piece; pinch bottom ends together. Repeat with the other pieces of dough. Place braids on a lightly greased baking sheet.

4. To make the glaze, beat egg yolk with water until foamy; stir in honey until well mixed. Evenly brush braids with the mixture, making sure to get into the folds and down the sides. Sprinkle tops evenly with sesame or poppy seeds (if using). Set in warm place uncovered for 1 hour, until doubled.

5. While loaves are rising, preheat oven to 400 degrees. Bake until shiny and golden brown and a wooden pick inserted into the center of the loaves comes out clean, 25 to 30 minutes. Remove from oven and let sit on pans for 5 minutes before carefully moving to a wire cooling rack. The long loaves will be very fragile; use a spatula when transferring.

The Symbolic Shapes of Challah

Challah, the delicious, rich egg bread found on Sabbath and holiday tables in Jewish homes, is steeped in religious traditions reaching back more than four thousand years. Hebrew law dictates the quantity of flour should be "no less than the weight of forty-three and one-fifth eggs," or three and a half pounds.

The loaves have a different shape for every occasion, each indicative of a specific meaning or importance:

On *Shabbat* (Sabbath—Friday nights), the loaves are braided with three, four, or six strands, meant to look like intertwined arms, symbolizing love. Three braids are symbolic of truth, peace, and justice. One large loaf braided into twelve humps or two small loaves of six represent the miracle of the twelve loaves for the twelve tribes of Israel.

For *Rosh Hashanah,* the round loaves—a circle with no beginning and no end—are symbolic of continuity.

At *Yom Kippur,* ladder shapes are eaten before the start of fasting to represent the promise of reaching great heights.

On *Purim,* two unshelled, hard-cooked eggs are baked into round loaves or the dough is shaped into small triangles, representing the eyes and ears of Hamman, minister to the king of the Persian Empire, who failed in his attempt to kill all Jews in Persia in early Biblical times.

On *Shavuot,* two oblong loaves are placed side by side on the table to resemble the Tablets of the Law given to Moses by God.

PANETTONE

[makes 1 large loaf]

This version of the rich, butter and egg Italian Christmas bread studded with fruit and nuts is a little more conservative in both ingredients and construction than most traditional panettone. Some of the usual components were either unaffordable or unavailable during the first part of the last century in northern Minnesota, but the resourceful Iron Range Italian immigrants made do. It wouldn't have been a true *Tavola Natale* without the high buttery round loaf rising from its traditional buttery paper robe.

* * *

You'll need roughly two days to prepare this bread, so making it over an early December weekend—in a double or triple batch so you'll have extra—might not be a bad idea. It freezes very well, and leftovers can be translated into delightful Anglo-Italo bread puddings and delicious Franco-Italo toasts for midwinter brunches. Begin the night before you plan to bake by making a *biga*—the Italian version of a sponge—and let it rest for twelve hours to ensure good rise and light texture. This method is the perfect place to use a bread machine. If you don't have a bread machine, make your dough using a hand mixer or a stand mixer with the dough hook attachment. The candied lemon peel and citron are available in most grocery stores before Christmas and in some Italian specialty stores year round. This version layers one piece of plain dough with one loaded with fruit and nuts and uses a tube or angel food cake pan with straight sides so the bread will rise; it won't work in a fluted or Bundt-style pan.

BIGA

1½ cups bread flour

½ cup cool water

⅛ teaspoon quick-rise yeast

2 tablespoons salted butter, at room temperature

DOUGH

½ cup warm water
(105–115 degrees)

1 packet (2 teaspoons) quick-rise yeast

white sugar

4–4½ cups bread flour, divided

12 tablespoons (1½ sticks) unsalted butter, at room temperature

1½ teaspoons kosher or sea salt

3 large eggs plus 3 large egg yolks, at room temperature, lightly beaten

1 teaspoon vanilla

½ cup golden raisins, plumped in light rum or white wine, drained, and patted dry

½ cup coarsely chopped candied lemon peel

½ cup coarsely chopped citron

½ cup blanched slivered almonds

25 whole blanched almonds

1. *The night before baking:* Make the biga by combining flour, water, and yeast. Knead briefly to moisten flour and activate yeast; dough will be stiff. If you're using a bread machine, allow the dough to knead for 5 minutes, then cancel the cycle. Grease a deep, narrow bowl with the butter; add the dough, rotate to coat, cover with a dish towel, and set aside in a moderately heated place or unheated oven (65–70 degrees) and allow to rise overnight, about 12 hours. It should be light and filled with bubbles by morning.

2. *The next morning:* Place the warm water in a small bowl, sprinkle on the yeast, stir in 1 teaspoon sugar, and sprinkle ½ cup flour over the top. Cover with plastic wrap and set aside in a warm place (80–85 degrees) for 5 to 10 minutes, until it begins to bubble.

3. While sponge is proofing, place butter in bowl of stand mixer fitted with paddle attachment, add ½ cup sugar, and beat until smooth; stir salt into beaten eggs and mix into butter. Exchange the paddle attachment for a dough hook. Add the sponge, vanilla, and 3½ to 4 cups flour, 1 cup at a time. Mix until dough becomes too stiff to take any more flour; turn out onto a floured surface and work in remaining flour by hand. Knead for 5 minutes, and divide dough in half; shape each piece into a round and place one in a buttered bowl; cover with plastic wrap and set aside to rise until doubled, about 1 hour.

4. Lightly dust the fruit and slivered almonds with some of the flour left from the kneading. Pat out the remaining dough into a small circle, sprinkle with the fruit and slivered almonds, and knead until thoroughly mixed. Place in a second buttered bowl, cover, and let rise until doubled, about 1 hour.

5. While dough pieces are rising, butter the sides and bottoms of the tube pan and sprinkle with 2–3 tablespoons sugar, turning pan to coat inside surface. Press whole almonds into the bottom of the pan, spacing evenly. When dough is ready, punch down and turn out each piece and knead separately for 3 or 4 minutes.

>>

6. Pat each piece into a triangle and roll out until 18–20 inches on one side and 10–12 inches on the other two. Lay the piece with fruit on top of the plain, slightly pinch long edges together, and roll toward the top of the short sides. Fit into the prepared pan, with the ends overlapping enough to equal the thickest part of the roll. Cover with plastic wrap and set aside in a warm place until doubled, about 45 minutes.

7. Preheat oven to 400 degrees. Bake for 10 minutes, then reduce heat to 350 degrees and bake for another 40 to 50 minutes, until an inserted wooden pick comes out clean and dry. Remove from oven and turn out onto a cooling rack, tapping the bottom to release any almonds stuck to the pan; press loose nuts back into the loaf while it is still warm. Dust top with additional sugar if desired. Slice in wedges when cool.

Cook's Notes: *If using a bread machine, you'll be limited to single batches, but you can save time by combining all the ingredients directly into the machine, following the manufacturer's directions. Serve panettone with a fortified red Italian wine.*

GRANDMA JESSIE'S HOT CROSS BUNS

[makes 12 large or 24 small buns]

My English grandmother wasn't much of a cook. Not to say she was a bad one, but she was the youngest of five girls in a family of eight children, and the tasks of daily meal preparation were handled by her older sisters. She did, however, know how to bake, which would come in handy when she had seven children of her own, all boys. My father grew up eating large, slightly sweet, soft white rolls dunked in hot cocoa for breakfast almost every morning—except on Easter Sunday. On Easter, she added saffron and currants to the dough and turned the everyday white rolls into hot cross buns, with crosses painted on the tops in confectioners' sugar icing.

When my dad married my mom, the morning cocoa ritual came with him, but the fluffy, just-out-of-the-oven rolls remained in my grandmother's kitchen until her youngest son left for college in the early 1950s. But she kept up her Easter Sunday tradition and had a linen napkin–lined basket filled with warm, saffron-currant buns waiting on the table if we were having dinner at her house, or she'd bring the buns and frosting to our house, where I got to help embellish their shiny, yellow tops with glistening white crosses.

• • •

My grandmother always spread the saffron on a pie tin and dried it for a few minutes in a "slow" oven to intensify the flavor, saying, "It's very expensive; if you heat it up first and crumble it in the warm milk, you'll make the flavor go farther."

Using a quick-rise yeast and making a sponge with bread flour and a pinch of sugar will shorten the process considerably and ensure a better rise. As always, read through the recipe steps before starting. These rolls should be light and fluffy; the dough is made in two steps, using only part of the flour in the first rise. If too much is added the dough will be heavy and dense. And—depending on humidity—the dough may not take up all the flour; don't try to use the full amount.

1 tablespoon saffron threads

SPONGE

⅓ cup warm whole milk (105–115 degrees)

1 packet (2 teaspoons) quick-rise yeast

pinch white sugar

1 tablespoon bread flour

DOUGH

1 cup whole milk or half-and-half

8 tablespoons (1 stick) salted butter, at room temperature

1 cup dried currants

2 large eggs, at room temperature

⅓ cup white sugar

1 teaspoon kosher or sea salt

4 cups bread flour, divided

1 large egg beaten with 1 tablespoon whole milk

ICING

1½–2 tablespoons half-and-half

1 cup confectioners' sugar, sifted

1. Preheat oven to 150 degrees or lowest setting. Sprinkle saffron threads on a baking sheet and place in oven to dry for 15 to 20 minutes.

2. To make the sponge: Place ⅓ cup warm milk in a glass measuring cup or bowl, sprinkle on yeast, followed by the sugar, then 1 tablespoon flour. Cover with plastic wrap and set in a warm place for 15 to 20 minutes, or until bubbling.

>>

3. Heat 1 cup milk or half-and-half to at least 110 degrees; stir in softened butter and cool to lukewarm. Remove saffron from oven and grind in a mortar and pestle or in a bowl with the back of a spoon; add to warm milk along with the currants. Turn off oven. Transfer sponge and warm milk to a large bowl.

4. In a small bowl, beat eggs well with the ⅓ cup sugar and salt, and add to sponge and milk. Stir in 2 cups of flour; continue stirring vigorously, at least 125 strokes, until the dough is thick and glossy. Cover bowl with plastic wrap and place in the cooling oven or another warm place (80–85 degrees) until doubled, about 1 hour.

5. Stir dough and begin adding ¾ cup of remaining flour. Sprinkle remaining 1¼ cups flour on a work surface or countertop, turn out dough and knead until it is smooth and elastic, 8 to 10 minutes. Work dough into a 24-inch-long roll; cut into 12 (2-inch) or 24 (1-inch) pieces. Shape by cupping your hands over two pieces at a time and rolling into balls on the floured surface. Place evenly spaced on 2 lightly greased baking sheets; cover with parchment or waxed paper, and set in a warm place until doubled, 20 to 30 minutes.

6. Preheat oven to 375 degrees. Brush tops with egg wash; use kitchen shears or a sharp knife to cut an X into the top of each roll. Bake small buns 10–15 minutes; large buns 15–20 minutes. Remove from oven and cool on baking sheet. Stir half-and-half into confectioners' sugar until smooth; wrap in a parchment paper cone or place in a zip-top bag; keep at room temperature. When ready to make crosses, snip a small piece from the end of the paper or a corner of the bag. Pipe into X marks on the cooled buns. Serve slightly warm or at room temperature with sweet unsalted butter.

Cook's Notes: Leftover rolls filled with leftover Easter ham make terrific sandwiches; add a dollop of coarse-ground mustard, a dill pickle, and a chilled ginger ale or beer. At Christmas, this dough makes a lovely braided wreath: tuck lightly toasted, slivered almonds and glacéed cherries into the seams before baking and add a few to the top of the icing.

CHAPTER 2

Breakfasts

When we came in then, with our pail of milk,
she'd have the fire going in the stove
and the oatmeal cooking for our breakfast;
everything would be ready for us.

ANNA LINNEA ELIASON,
AGE NINETY-FIVE, LITTLE SWAN, OUTSIDE HIBBING, MINNESOTA

*E*ach culture had their own take on breakfast, which in part reflected the climate of their country or region of origin. Over time, people's eating habits changed as they adapted to physical work demands, the often harsh northern Minnesota winter weather, and unfamiliar foods in place of those of their homelands, which were no longer available to them.

For the southern Europeans from areas close to the balmy Mediterranean and Adriatic Seas, fresh produce had been available for most if not the entire year, and breakfast was a lighter meal—usually coffee, bread, fruit, and cheese. The weather and menu differences weren't so radical for the Scandinavians and northern Europeans, who'd come from a similar climate and began their mornings with hearty grain- and protein-based meals. Swedes and Norwegians—who were more likely farmers than miners—typically saved their version of the modest southern European morning repast for a midmorning coffee break or a light evening lunch, eaten several hours after supper.

First-shift miners needed to be out of the house at an early hour, which meant wives were up even earlier than their husbands, preparing breakfasts and lunch pails in the predawn hours at the start of their day in the kitchen, a day that would end twelve to fourteen hours later. The same held true for wives whose husbands worked the twelve-hour night (second) shift; breakfast needed to be ready when those miners arrived home in the wee morning hours. The fire in the stove would be lit; bread, set to rise the night before, baked; eggs (if there were chickens) gathered; big pots of oatmeal or porridge, enough to feed the entire family, cooked—all before anyone else had opened their eyes. Daughters who'd reached early adolescence were often enlisted to help their mothers in the predawn hours, a preparatory course for what lay ahead in their lives. The exceptions were farm families, where everyone had a hand in the multiple morning chores that needed to be done while it was still dark. These rounds of duty started at a young age, and those youngsters worked up appetites for breakfasts that often seemed like banquets when compared to those eaten by their counterparts in town.

Still, when it came to breakfast, a number of commonalities existed among the different ethnic groups, with the differences found in the preparations. There were grain-based dishes in the forms of hot cereals, pancakes, and breads; proteins like cultured yogurt-like milk, cheese, eggs, bacon, sausages, and ham; all these rounded out by fried potatoes or hashes combining eggs with leftover meats, gravies, and potatoes.

Most breakfasts were served family style with platters of food and baskets of bread placed on the table and passed by the diners, or, when space was an issue, they were plated and served from the stove, usually by the mother. The Scandinavians get the nod for introducing the idea of breakfast as a buffet–brunch into the American recipe playbook with their long-standing, shared-meal tradition of the *smörgåsbord.*

CREAMY OVERNIGHT WINTER OATMEAL

[serves 6]

This is an updated version of the oatmeal the Suomu sisters, Linda and Lila, were in charge of making daily on the wood-burning kitchen stove while they were growing up on a large dairy farm outside of Cherry, a small Finnish enclave in rural St. Louis County. The sister assigned to the night chores had to soak the hard oats in milk and water in the big pot before setting the table for breakfast, getting the bread into its first rising, setting up the coffeepot for the morning, and damping the overnight fire in the kitchen stove to a slow and steady heat source. The very last thing she would do was put a cinnamon stick in the pot with the oats, make sure the lid wasn't on too tight, and push the pot to the back corner of the flat cooktop, away from the hottest area, where it could slowly simmer overnight.

The next day, the sister who had the early morning chores would bring the fire back up to a blaze, punch down the bread, shape it into loaves, cover them, and set them to rise again, put the coffeepot on the stove to cook, get some water going for soft-boiled eggs, and warm some milk to stir into the oatmeal—which by then was fairly thick—along with some raisins or apples and maybe some nuts. While the oatmeal was cooking, she'd get the *viili* (page 50) down from the top of the cupboard, where it had been thickening since breakfast the day before, and set it on the table, along with a basket of hardtack (page 18) from the tin box out in the back porch. By the time her father, mother, and brother, who had been up even earlier than she was, came in from the barn with fresh eggs from the chickens and milk from the cows, the oatmeal would be done, the coffee percolating away, and the bread ready to pop into the oven. The very last things she had to do before sitting down herself was drop the fresh eggs into the simmering water and grab the butter, Squeaky Cheese (page 104), and cream for the coffee out of the icebox.

* * *

While most of us don't have a wood-burning stove in our kitchens to gradually cook oatmeal overnight, we can make it in a slow cooker, which is almost as good. Using a combination of steel-cut and rolled oats will help the cereal develop a creamy consistency as it cooks. Steel-cut oats are very hard; soak them in warm water for 15 minutes with the slow cooker on high before stirring in the other ingredients. Add only a pinch of salt at first; the longer something cooks, the saltier it becomes. You can add more to the finished dish if you want.

1½ cups steel-cut oats

1 cup warm water

¾–1 cup rolled oats
(not quick oats)

6 cups whole milk

1 cinnamon stick

2 tablespoons salted butter

½ cup dried apples, or 1 cup fresh

½ cup dried apricots, or 1 cup fresh

¼ cup raisins

salt

½ cup walnuts, toasted and chopped, optional

brown sugar, optional

1. Set slow cooker to high; add steel-cut oats and water, cover, and cook for 10 to 15 minutes; pot should be simmering. Remove cover, stir, and add rolled oats, milk, cinnamon stick, butter, dried fruits (if using fresh fruit, hold out until near the end), and a pinch of salt. Stir, put cover on, turn heat to low, turn off the lights, and go to bed.

2. In the morning, uncover, stir, and taste for salt and texture. Turn heat to high and add more milk or water, warmed, if needed, and adjust salt to taste. Add fresh fruit and nuts, if desired. Serve with milk and brown sugar.

Cook's Notes: *In winter, make a large pot, or enough for several days, early in the week and heat in individual portions in the mornings. It's a timesaver, and a great way to have a quick, high-energy breakfast that will stay with you up until lunch.*

VIILI / **FINNISH YOGURT**

[serves 2–3]

Viili, a Finnish live-culture yogurt, was a breakfast staple in kitchens on Iron Range Swede-Finn dairy farms in the early to mid-twentieth century. Phonetically pronounced *vē'elie,* the colloquial pronunciation in many Scandinavian homes was heard as *fēel'ya.*

"You have to have some real good sour milk to start; milk from yesterday is best," my cousin Linnea Eliason told me.

Our milk wasn't pasteurized and it worked good; you can't make it with pasteurized milk, it doesn't set right. And it has to be covered and in a warm place where it can sit overnight, but not too warm or it will break and be runny instead of thick and smooth. Ours was made from an old, old starter; older than I was even when I first started eating it. When you brought your spoon out of the bowl it had long strings, almost like shiny liquid ribbons. My mother said that meant it was good for us, with lots of healthy bacteria in it.

We'd put them in our colored bowls we used to get in hundred-pound flour sacks, and cover them with coffee saucers that fit just right. Those came in the flour too, and we had every color they made: yellow, red, blue, turquoise, and green. When we got up in the mornings, we always went to the barn to milk first thing. When we came in then, with our pail of milk still warm from the cows to give to our mother, she'd have the fire going in the stove and the coffee and the oatmeal cooking for our breakfast; everything would be ready for us. Then she would take those colored bowls down from the top of the cabinet where it was warmest in winter, and yesterday's *viili* would be all set and ready for us to have with our breakfast. In summer she'd have to put those bowls on a shelf in the pantry because the kitchen would be too hot from the fire in the stove.

She'd lift a spoonful of the *viili* from one of the bowls then put that in a clean pitcher, then pour some of the milk we brought in—right from the barn and still warm from the cows!—stir that up lil' bit and pour it into some more of those colored bowls; then she'd cover those with coffee saucers and put 'em right back up on top of the cabinet to be ready for our breakfast tomorrow.

• • •

Viili is easy to make at home, just as Linnea described it: combine a bit of today's *viili* with warm milk for tomorrow's; cover and set in a warm place for twenty-four hours. The only differences are your culture likely came from a commercially made yogurt, although heirloom starters are available online (search for "viili" or "active yogurt cultures") or possibly from an organic dairy farm; and the milk you'll be using probably won't have come straight from the barn, still warm from the cows. Sadly, you'll have to use a modern method—like a microwave—to heat it, but putting it in bright-colored bowls might make it taste like it came from yesterday's morning milking.

1 tablespoon starter	1½ cups whole or 2 percent milk

1. Place starter in the bottom of a ceramic bowl that will hold 2 cups of liquid. Heat milk to lukewarm, pour over the starter, and stir to mix. Cover with a saucer or with loose plastic wrap; let stand at room temperature, away from excessive heat or cold, for 24 hours.

2. Remove several tablespoons to make a new batch. Serve at room temperature, or chill if preferred.

Cook's Notes: *Use* viili *in place of some of the liquid in sourdough bread and pancakes; blend into smoothies and salad dressings; mix in fresh berries or granola. It's a very healthy addition to your breakfast routine.*

SVENSK PANNKAKOR / SWEDISH PANCAKES

[serves 6]

Every Christmas morning while I was growing up—and long into adulthood—my mother made the same breakfast her mother had made on Christmas when she, her sister, and three brothers were growing up, with one notable exception: no lingonberry sauce. Lingonberries were unknown on the Iron Range until the last half of the twentieth century, and even then were only available as preserves, never as frozen berries outright. So Grandma Johnson did what her fellow Swede-Finns did: she used cranberries.

* * *

Swedish tradition almost mandates these delicate, small, crêpe-like pancakes be served each week with Lingonberry Sauce (page 53) following the customary weekly Thursday Pea Soup supper (page 120). They're fast and easy to prepare; they make a delicious brunch or lunch buffet dessert; and they're perfect at Christmas or any time of the year. So why restrict them to one day a week?

In Sweden the cakes are made on a *plattpanna,* a special cast-iron pan with seven shallow indentations, allowing you to make multiple pancakes at once. Available in specialty cookware shops and online, the pan is not an imperative. The batter is thin and the pancakes are small, and they're so rich no additional butter is needed when serving, but the pink-tinged cumulus cloud–like whipped cream, so sweet and soft in the mouth—now that's imperative.

3 large eggs	1 cup all-purpose flour
¼ teaspoon sea or kosher salt	1¾ cups whole milk
½ teaspoon white sugar	Lingonberry Sauce [page 53]
8 tablespoons (1 stick) unsalted butter, melted in a glass measuring cup	whipped heavy cream, unsweetened, optional

1. Preheat oven to 200 degrees and put plates in oven to warm. In a large bowl, whisk eggs and add salt and sugar, whisking to blend. Stir in 4 tablespoons of the melted butter; set remainder aside. Add flour in three steps, alternating with the milk. Stir with whisk until very smooth. Pour into a 1-quart glass measuring cup or a pitcher.

2. Warm a cast-iron pan or skillet over medium heat; test with drops of water: when a drop bounces and boils off, the pan is ready. Pour 1 teaspoon of the reserved melted butter in the center of the pan, turning the pan to evenly coat the surface. Pour a scant ⅓ cup of batter into the center of the pan; quickly swirl to evenly coat the surface. Cook until the pancake sets, 1 to 1½ minutes. Gently insert a rubber spatula under an edge of the pancake—don't gouge or tear—and carefully lift the pancake by the edges and turn; cook until lightly golden on the other side, 15 to 30 seconds. Transfer to a plate in the warm oven. If the first pancake seems too thick, thin the batter slightly with warm water. Repeat with the remaining butter and batter to make about 12 pancakes.

3. Fold pancakes into quarters or roll them up; serve with lingonberry sauce and a dollop of whipped cream (if using).

Cook's Notes: *You can also prepare the batter in a blender, adding all the ingredients at once and processing until smooth. A well-seasoned cast-iron pan is the best surface for cooking these pancakes, but a nonstick or buttered stainless steel skillet will work, too. This is the perfect recipe for using a warming drawer if you have one. The pancakes will remain moist, warm, and easy to fold or roll. Set the temperature gauge on its lowest setting or to 150 degrees. Don't be intimidated by the cooking specifics; after flipping your second pancake, you'll be a pro.*

LINGONBERRY SAUCE

[makes about 1 quart]

Lingonberries* are small, tart wild berries found throughout the Scandinavian countries, where they appear as preserves and sauces, in puddings, on pancakes, and alongside many meat dishes, especially Swedish Meatballs (page 81). Though the climate was comparable to that of Scandinavia, they didn't grow on the Iron Range. So those resourceful Scandinavians substituted cranberries, which they found to be similar in tartness and flavor and always available around Christmas—but they just weren't the same.

*Lingon in Swedish; tyttebær in Norwegian and Danish; rauðber in Icelandic; and puolukka in Finnish.

Before the Internet and Ikea, lingonberries could sometimes be found in Scandinavian specialty shops, but usually as jams or jellies, and far outside of the Iron Range. My mother was thrilled to find some frozen without sugar at Ingebretsen's in Minneapolis on a summer trip to visit cousins during the early 1960s; and my grandmother, who hadn't had any lingonberries since immigrating to the United States in 1914, was pretty happy, too.

Established in a South Minneapolis Swedish enclave in 1921, Ingebretsen's is still a main source of ingredients specific to Scandinavian cooking, including house-made potato sausage.

Christmas mornings in our house had always meant sour cream waffles or Swedish Pancakes (page 51) and Swedish potato sausages. Now we could have the complete Christmas menu, including *lingon*berry sauce!

• • •

The sauce is simple: three ingredients (one of which is water), made in one step that takes ten minutes. Thaw the lingonberries so they release their juice before cooking. Besides waffles and pancakes, meatballs and puddings, this sauce is a good accompaniment or glaze for roasted poultry, pork, and salmon. To customize your sauce, consider adding a few whole cloves, a cinnamon stick, or a piece of orange rind; remove before serving.

Lingonberries are high in pectin and will thicken with less sugar than other berries; the sugar-to-water ratio for sweetness and thickness can be adjusted to your personal preference.

1–1½ cups white sugar

¼–½ cup warm water

4 cups thawed lingonberries with their juice

2–3 whole cloves or 1 stick cinnamon or 1 large piece orange rind, optional

1. Place 1 cup sugar in a 1½–2 quart saucepan, add ¼ cup warm water, and stir to dissolve. Add thawed lingonberries and their juice, rinsing container with a little warm water to remove all juice. Place pan over high heat, bring to a boil, and reduce heat to a simmer. Add any optional ingredients, and simmer for 10 minutes, or until thickened to preference. Taste and add more sugar or water as desired.

2. If not using immediately, chill with optional ingredients still in the sauce; remove these before serving. Cover and store in the refrigerator; the sauce will keep indefinitely.

ITALIAN FRITTATA

[serves 4–6]

Oven-baked and served directly from the pan, Italian frittata is a rustic, farm-house take on the more refined French omelet. Miners often carried leftover wedges wrapped in brown or waxed paper in their lunch pails or pockets with a crust of bread for a little midday pick-me-up. The same holds true today, with a little salad and a small glass of red wine added for extra flavor and an energy boost.

1 tablespoon olive oil	kosher salt, to taste
12 ounces pancetta, finely chopped	pinch freshly grated nutmeg, optional
12 ounces yellow onion, finely chopped	generous pinch red pepper flakes, optional
8 extra-large eggs	8 ounces baby spinach leaves
½ cup whole milk, at room temperature	1 cup grated provolone or whole milk mozzarella or a combination

1. Preheat oven to 450 degrees. Heat olive oil in a large cast-iron or ovenproof skillet over medium heat, add pancetta and onions, and cook until slightly brown; remove from heat.

2. Beat eggs in a large bowl with a wire whisk until blended, slowly stir in milk, then beat vigorously until frothy; beat in salt, nutmeg, and pepper (if using). Pour into hot pan, and spread evenly by tilting the pan; don't stir.

3. Toss together spinach and cheese, and sprinkle over eggs. Turn burner to medium, and cook for a few minutes, just until eggs begin to set on the bottom and sides. Place in middle of preheated oven, and bake for 10 to 15 minutes, until eggs are cooked; they should be slightly puffed and lightly browned.

4. Remove from oven to a trivet, cut into wedges, and serve from the pan.

Cook's Notes: *Serve with a green salad dressed with a simple olive oil and red wine vinegar dressing and some crostini, even for breakfast!*

CHAPTER 3

Dinners

"Let's go to Ting Town tonight!"
was what legions of Hibbing, Chisholm,
and Side Lake kids were waiting
to hear their mom or dad say.

TING TOWN: TALE OF A LOVE'S LABOR LOST

Dinner on the Range was the midday meal, which in current times is lunch, whereas the meal after what most would call dinner was referred to as lunch. Just as "Sunday dinner" referred to the big meal of the day eaten following morning church services, during the week dinner was the main meal of the day. This tradition was likely influenced by the schedule of the typical farmer, who, rising before sunrise, might have already put in six hours by the time the sun reached its highpoint and was in need of some serious refueling. This routine also worked well for the equally early rising, hard-laboring miners.

With the lion's share of their energy spent before the midday meal, neither farmers nor miners were interested in eating a heavy meal between the end of their workday and the beginning of their sleep. So that left supper, which typically meant a more casual table and lighter fare than the traditional definition for dinner indicated. Supper was served in the evening, in that time slot others called dinner. Confused? You might want to sleep on it, after you have lunch.

PASTIES

[serves 6 hungry people]

The Cornish were among the earliest arrivals at the Iron Range mines, coming by way of Michigan. Their small physical stature coupled with their experience working in the old, narrow, underground copper and tin mines of Cornwall made them perfect candidates for the Michigan copper mines in the late nineteenth century, but it wasn't long before Michigan's mines were far overstaffed and the workers far underpaid. News of open-ended opportunities in northern Minnesota in the early 1900s easily lured them to the Iron Range, where their size and skill set were once again readily welcomed. Their work ethic was admirable, but by far their most important contribution to the growing communities wasn't an ability to work for long hours while confined in small underground spaces; it was the traditional Cornish miner's lunch they carried down the shafts every day, tightly wrapped in their pockets: the pasty.

· · ·

This Cornish tradition was quickly adopted by other immigrant arrivals, and church ladies across the Range followed suit, making and delivering hot pasties to sell to miners at lunchtimes. Eventually everyone wanted in, so schedules were worked out, and these evolved into unofficial congregational competitions as different variations began to be developed. The most notable is probably the Finnish version of rutabagas in place of carrots or sometimes potatoes. Some find this root vegetable's strong flavor to be overwhelming; grating the rutabaga adds a hint rather than a wallop of the earthy taste. Some sift the flour and others add baking powder to give lift to the flaky pastry. A few add gravy while others merely enclose a pat of butter. Some say to mix the filling and some insist layering is best, with potatoes on the bottom to absorb the juices from the meat in the middle and butter on the top of the vegetables. This version uses the latter technique.

4½ cups sifted all-purpose flour, divided

salt

¾ teaspoon baking powder

1 cup chilled vegetable shortening or lard or a combination

½ cup ice water

freshly ground pepper

>>

2 cups sirloin or top round cut into ¾-inch pieces

2 cups yellow onions cut into ¾-inch pieces

2 cups red potatoes, peeled and cut into ¾-inch pieces

1½ cups carrots, peeled and cut into ¾-inch pieces

1½ cups grated rutabaga, optional (see head note)

2 tablespoons salted butter

1 large egg yolk mixed with ¼ cup water

1. Mix 4 cups flour, 1 tablespoon salt, and baking powder in a large bowl. Add the shortening, cutting it in with a pastry blender or two forks. Sprinkle ice water over the mixture a little at a time, toss with a fork, then work in by hand; add more if needed so the dough is easy to handle. Divide the dough into 6 pieces, wrap in waxed paper or plastic wrap, and refrigerate for 30 minutes. Season remaining ½ cup flour with salt and pepper to taste and add chopped beef and onions; toss to coat.

2. Preheat oven to 425 degrees. Roll pieces of dough into 8-inch circles on a lightly floured surface. On one half of each circle, half an inch from the edge, layer about 2 heaping tablespoons of potatoes, 2 heaping tablespoons of beef and onions mixture, and about ¼ cup each of carrots and rutabaga (if using); add salt and pepper after each addition if desired. Dot the top of each with 1½ teaspoons butter. Moisten the edges of the dough with water and fold over, forming a half moon. Press the edges together to seal, and crimp with your fingertips or press down with the tines of a fork.

3. Use a spatula to slide pasties onto a lightly greased or parchment-covered baking sheet; leave a good inch between each pasty. Brush the tops with the egg yolk–water mixture and make several small slashes in the top of each with a sharp knife.

4. Bake for 30 minutes; reduce heat to 350 degrees and bake for another 30 minutes, until the pasties are nicely browned.

Cook's Notes: *These freeze extremely well before baking; you may want to re-slash the top of the crust. Bake directly from the freezer starting at 300 degrees for 30 minutes; increase temperature to 375 degrees and bake for an additional 35 to 45 minutes, until golden brown and the internal temperature is 165 degrees. Serve hot or at room temperature in the traditional Iron Range style: with ketchup.*

An Ecumenical Lunch

Historical records from the 1920s and '30s list the weekly church pasty sale schedule, one religiously followed at the Hull-Rust-Mahoning Mine in North Hibbing:

Mondays: Immaculate Conception, the Little Italian Catholic church: *beef and pork*

Tuesdays: Grace Lutheran, the Finnish church: *rutabagas instead of potatoes*

Wednesdays: First Presbyterian Church: *carrots, potatoes, and gravy*

Thursdays: First Lutheran, the Swedish church: *onions, carrots, potatoes; no gravy*

Fridays: Wesley Methodist Church: *carrots, potatoes, and gravy*

Unfortunately, no written record was made as to whose pasties were most preferred by miners, so we'll just have to rely on hearsay.

SOUTH AMERICANS

[makes 32 sandwiches]

While the origin of this seemingly southern recipe is hard to pin down, its east Iron Range history is well documented; just ask any seasoned barkeeper around Virginia, Eveleth, Biwabik, or Aurora–Hoyt Lakes, where these spicy ground meat and vegetable sandwiches were tavern staples. Big batches were made weekly and were always available to the patrons who ate them in preparation for a night of heavy imbibing—and as a morning-after curative. Most recipes were twice the size of the one that follows, with double the amount of oil, which has been considerably cut back here. The mixture freezes very well and is great to have on hand for Minnesota midwinter get-togethers, but if this recipe is still too big, you can make half with equally satisfying results.

. . .

You'll need one very large skillet or saucepan to accommodate all the ingredients. Use the pulse mode on your food processor to grind the salt pork and pepperoni, and pulse-grind the vegetables in the order given, emptying the bowl after processing each addition. *A word of caution*: never touch your eyes or face while handling hot peppers! Just a speck of oil from your fingers to your face will make your skin burn like crazy, so wash your hands with *lots* of good soap and hot water when you're finished.

½–1 cup canola oil	1 bunch celery, roughly chopped
¼ pound salt pork, ground or finely chopped	1½ pounds yellow onions, roughly chopped
½ pound pepperoni, sliced or cubed	½ pound cremini mushrooms, optional
1 pound lean ground beef	2–3 fresh jalapeño peppers, seeded and finely chopped, or 1 (4-ounce) can pickled jalapeño or other hot peppers
1 pound ground pork	
1½ pounds green bell peppers, roughly chopped	
1 pound red bell peppers, roughly chopped	salt and pepper
	1 bunch curly parsley, finely chopped
4 pounds green tomatoes, roughly chopped	1 head escarole or endive, finely chopped
4 pounds red, ripe tomatoes, roughly chopped	Italian bread

1. Heat ½ cup canola oil in a very large skillet or saucepan over medium, add salt pork, and cook for several minutes, until slightly browned. While salt pork is browning, use the pulse mode on your food processor to grind the pepperoni. Add to salt pork; stir to combine. Add ground beef and pork, breaking up into small pieces, and add remaining ½ cup of oil if mixture seems dry. Cook over medium heat until all meat is evenly browned.

2. While the meats are cooking, pulse-grind the vegetables in the order given up through the jalapeños, emptying the bowl into the skillet after processing each. Simmer for 2 to 3 hours, tasting several times for heat and salt. Add salt to taste, and pepper if more heat is desired.

3. Remove from heat, stir in chopped parsley and escarole or endive, taste for seasoning and adjust as needed, and serve on sliced Italian bread—with a large side of paper napkins!

Ting Town: Tale of a Love's Labor Lost

From 1930 through the early 1970s, something happened late each spring that mid–Iron Range kids of all ages had been waiting for since school had begun the previous fall. Not summer vacation; something almost better than that. Ting Town opened! On a small triangular tract of land at the intersection of Highway 5 and County Road 132, right smack between Hibbing and Chisholm, stood the eight-sided, orange pavilion of northern Minnesota–style barbecue pleasure. Opened in 1930 by Elmer and Rose Portugue of Chisholm, "Ting Town Drive Inn" is said to have been Minnesota's first drive-in restaurant. Where the idea for the place and the name came from, no one seems to know; back then, especially for those who knew and grew up with Ting Town, that didn't matter. It had always been there, and it meant magic.

Ting Town was open for just the short months of summer between Memorial Day and Labor Day. Service started at four and ended promptly at midnight, and the only identifying sign anywhere was the long, half fire-breathing/half grinning white, sea serpent–like figure perched along the southwest edge of the roof. Tilted, time-faded charcoal gray letters ran down its back and tail proclaiming: TING TOWN and BARBECUE. There was no running water or heat inside, and outside there was no place to put trash. The only amenities were electricity, a little propane stove, an old refrigerator for soda pop, and an outdoor biffy across the parking lot at the edge of the woods. Bright yellow light bulbs poked out along the front edges of the generous eaves, driving the night bugs away and bathing the parking lot in a golden, welcoming light. Neat, bold, black-lettered signs above and beneath the windows instructed patrons on how the system worked: "PLEASE PAY WHEN SERVED." "HELP US AVOID SCATTERING PAPER." "TOOT-N-TELL-UM."

A few miles to the north, beyond the great granite walls of the Laurentian Divide that straddle Highway 5, are a number of pristine lakes that draw scores of area Iron Rangers to shorelines dotted with summer homes, campgrounds, and weekend-cottage getaways. People began making seasonal pilgrimages to their cabins and the camping and picnic areas at McCarthy Beach State Park around the same time the winter shutters came off the Ting Town windows. Right around Memorial Day, when yellow cowslips carpeted the ditches and the woods were edged in pink chokecherry and wild plum blossoms, barbecue season had arrived, and "Let's go to Ting Town tonight!" was what legions of Hibbing, Chisholm, and Side Lake kids were waiting to hear their mom or dad say.

Sunday nights on the way home from a weekend up at the lake, this was the place to stop for supper, and from late spring all through the summer, my brother and I sat in the backseat with fingers crossed and legs kicking as our car began its climb up the hulking gray Laurentian precipice on Highway 5. Right about there, Dad could usually be counted on to explain—once again—how the men had to blast dynamite right into the middle of this mountainous rock to make the road, which made driving through this part like being inside a giant, granite-walled canyon. Then he always added the part about how their pocket magnets went haywire in the process. And then he'd have to tell us—

>>

again—how this very spot determined which way the water under the ground went. If the rain fell on the north side of the road, it went up to Hudson Bay in Canada, but if it fell on the south side, it went down to the Gulf of Mexico. Right about there, we didn't care about Canada, Mexico, or magnets. What we cared about and wanted was a couple more miles in front of us, and we were hoping he'd notice our desperate situation and turn our aqua blue and white Studebaker station wagon into the Ting Town parking lot.

The sound of the engine slowing, the crunch of gravel beneath the wheels, and the smell of dry dirt mingled with the antiseptic odor emanating from hundreds of yellow tansy plants rimming the edges of the lot meant we were stopping. If all we heard was the continued sound of tires rotating on smooth asphalt with the occasional thump from a heat-heaved tar seam, we knew we were heading straight home, past the glowing yellow lights bidding us to turn in and that giant lizard on the roof, who sniggered at our misfortune as our car continued on by.

Driving by during winter was almost as bad. We could only gaze out of our frosted backseat window at the wonderful octagon of orange-painted lateral logs with its pointed snow-covered roof that now resembled a giant Dairy Queen cone. Long icicles often reached from the eaves all the way down to the parking lot, crystalline jail bars to keep winter and its intruders out. The sight almost always brought thoughts of warm summer nights and sweet or spicy meat sandwiches, so vivid you could almost smell and taste them; and Memorial Day was a long, long way away.

Though it was Elmer who had built the place, Ting Town was run by Rose. Through the years she staffed the stand with teenage girls from around her Chisholm neighborhood. To be selected as a Ting Town carhop held high summer status, and Rose—Mrs. Portugue to the girls—had strict standards: long hair had to be pulled back into a ponytail, short hair held down with barrettes; white shirts and black pants, nothing shorter than pedal pushers; and no makeup. Boys with carhop crushes and driver's licenses were known to hang out in the parking lot in hopes of free food or offering the object of their interest a lift home, but Rose had rules here as well: no idling engines; nothing on the house; we close at midnight; and no rides into town with anyone but her. She brought the girls out to the stand in her car, and she'd bring them back to town in it, too.

Ting Town was busy from the minute it opened each May, requiring new carhop initiates to quickly master walking across loose gravel while carrying overloaded trays of sandwiches and glass pop bottles, straws bobbing up out of their long clear, brown, or green necks, without spilling a drop. When they were really busy, especially Friday and Saturday nights, those girls didn't hop with their trays; they sprinted.

Clearly, Rose was a woman ahead of her time. Ting Town patrons got fast food before fast food had been heard of; drive-throughs hadn't been invented yet. By five or six every weekend, the parking lot would be filled with carloads of families stopping to get big bags of sandwiches to take up to the lake for dinner, even if it meant waiting for a few minutes with the radio tuned to WMFG. It was worth it. Every make of car—Packards to Bel Airs,

Caddies to Ramblers—could be seen in the parking lot over the course of the summer, especially on Friday date nights, when it was full from opening right up to closing. To us kids, this was better than a dress-up dinner at the Androy Hotel in Hibbing or Valentini's Supper Club in Chisholm any day.

The menu wasn't big, but it didn't need to be. Only three sandwiches were offered: beef, pork, or ham, all served on soft, white Master Bread buns; Orange Crush, Dad's Root Beer or Cream Soda, and 7-Up were the only beverage options. The cuts of meat Rose used were economical, fat laden, and full of flavor and had been slowly roasted in her basement kitchen. The bottom half of the bun was set on a large square of waxed paper by one of the inside ladies, slid along the counter where the meat of choice got heaped on top, and then crowned with the secret sauce by Rose, and only Rose, who wielded her ladle like a scepter. The next lady in line patted the top of the bun into place, pulled up the corners of the paper, and carefully wrapped the sandwich like a newborn baby in a receiving blanket. The precious bundles were placed in red waffle-weave plastic baskets, with dill pickle slices and Old Dutch potato chips tucked in at the side, and then set on metal trays with lots of extra napkins, essential for catching the delicious sauce that would ooze from between the buns when you peeled the waxed paper away and began to nibble in.

Within a ten-minute eternity of your dinner desires being made known, a silhouette behind the order window slid open the confessional-sized screen and passed a tray out to one of the BBQ acolytes waiting under the shadow of the eaves. The overloaded aluminum trays, with two little hooks for hanging from a car window and a rubber-tipped arm that folded down to the door as a brace, were promptly delivered to the driver's side, where the dad had rolled the window halfway up while waiting for the carhop to bring the food. People often ordered so many sandwiches that the hop would have to bring out the order on two trays; the second one was always delivered to the window on the mom's side of the car. And there it was: the thing you had been waiting all day, all weekend, all winter for. Putting your face down to one of those sandwiches was like bowing your head at the communion rail on Sunday. The smell alone was enough to make even the most stoic Norwegians swoon.

While the number of barbecue sandwiches Rose served each summer was staggering, it was her sauce that was legendary. For decades people tried to get her to reveal that recipe. Some even offered her money—a lot, as the story goes—but she wasn't handing it out to anybody. No one—not her family; not even the girls who worked at the stand, inside or out—knew the recipe. There were always those who claimed to have it; those who insisted they had figured it out; and those who were sure they could get it because they knew someone who knew someone who was a sister, or a second cousin, or one of Rose's neighbors three doors down.

"I've got the recipe. I got it from (here they'd fill in the name of someone you both knew), so you know it has to be the REAL recipe!"

During the 1960s into the early '70s, Twin Cities college potluck gatherings hosted by students from Chisholm and Hibbing often included one of the reputed versions. It was not uncommon to find these twenty-something Iron Rangers, plied with beer or some other recreational equivalent of the day, standing around food tables offering up

>>

serious evaluations, a sight subject to question by city kids, usually with raised eyebrows. In the end, the critical results were pretty much the same:

"No, not fatty enough. The fat needs to be soaked into the bun."

"Too much tomato sauce, or vinegar, or something."

"More onion."

"The meat is too thick. It needs to be thinner so it'll melt in your mouth."

"No. This isn't it. It's close, but definitely not it."

On and on, intent opinions were offered. These kids may not have been Craig Claibornes or Julia Childs, but they knew what they were talking about. This was a serious subject; this was Ting Town.

The closest I managed to get to the real recipe was from my Aunt Josephine, who'd been a carhop there in the late 1940s. The second-youngest in an Italian family of fourteen children, she'd gotten her job through one of her older sisters, Catherine, who was married and happened to be Rose's next-door neighbor. Auntie Jo rode with Rose out to the stand, sitting on the backseat with the aluminum foil–covered roaster ovens of hot beef, pork, and ham and pots of fragrant, warm barbecue sauce at her feet. She told me how Rose slowly roasted all the meats in those big, portable ovens, then pulled and shredded the beef and pork and shaved the ham off the bone into melt-in-your-mouth slivers. During the heat of summer this endeavor took place in the cool confines of her basement, which she'd outfitted with a stove.

It was said to be like a secret laboratory down there, and, with very few exceptions, no one was allowed in when the meats were roasting and that sauce was simmering. One of those exceptions was Auntie Jo's nephew Frank, and that was only after he had enrolled in the seminary in St. Paul. If he was home for a summer visit and Rose happened to spot Frank outside in his mother's backyard, she would open her kitchen door and wave him over with a "Hiya, Frankie. How about a little barbecue?" After all, he was going to be a priest, and you could count on a priest to keep a secret. Well, Frank didn't finish the seminary; he fell in love and got married. He didn't get the recipe either.

· · ·

On a subzero night in February 1974, some cold snowmobilers broke into the boarded-up octagon, built a fire to warm themselves up, and burned the place down. Summoned from her sleep, Rose, then a widow for twenty-five years, watched along with family, friends, and neighbors as her beloved forty-four-year-old landmark burned to the ground. Driving by the charred remains for the rest of that winter was enough to bring tears to anyone's eyes. In spring the building was razed, and Ting Town was gone for good. Except for two seasons during World War II, Ting Town had been open every summer since 1930. When Rose Portugue died in May 2000 at the age of eighty-seven, the secret to the name and the sauce passed away from us as well.

To this day it's doubtful that anyone who visited Ting Town as a child or an adult can drive past that sacred spot at the height of summer, its nearly vanished parking lot surrounded by tall stands of swaying yellow, button-headed tansy and blanketed by a quilt of purple and white clover, Shasta daisies, and Indian paintbrushes, without sighing for a moment over a true love lost.

Ting Town outside Chishom, Minnesota

Fraboni & Sons, Hibbing, Minnesota

PORKETTA

[serves 10]

This inexpensive, economical cut of pork had humble beginnings before being elevated to the status of one of the three essential Iron Range "Ps": Porketta, Pasties, and *Potica*. No stranger to area Italians who made their versions at home, porketta turned into a lunch and picnic staple for most all other ethnic groups in and beyond the mining region thanks largely to Leo Fraboni and the family sausage company founded by his father.

· · ·

Properly seasoning a porketta is important; getting the herbs and spices deep into all nooks and crannies is key, so boning the roast is essential—and never, ever trim any of the fat. If you don't know how to, or don't want to, bone a roast, ask the butcher to do it. Once seasoned, rolled, and tied, the meat is wrapped and refrigerated for at least twenty-four hours to become infused with all the flavors of the rub. While you're at it, why not make several and freeze a couple uncooked; they're great to have on hand, and the flavor will only improve.

1 (5-pound) pork butt or shoulder roast, boned

2 tablespoons kosher or coarse sea salt, or to taste

2 tablespoons freshly ground pepper, or to taste

1 tablespoon garlic powder, or to taste

3 tablespoons fennel seeds, toasted and finely ground in a mortar and pestle or spice mill

1 tablespoon extra-virgin olive oil

7–8 cloves garlic, minced

2 cups fresh fennel fronds, minced, or 2 tablespoons dried and crumbled

handful flat Italian parsley leaves, minced

Italian hard rolls

mustard, for serving

1. Lay pork roast on a rimmed baking sheet; open flat and dry all surfaces with several sheets of paper towel. In a small bowl, mix together salt, pepper, garlic powder, and ground fennel; remove 2 tablespoons and set aside. Mix the remaining 6 tablespoons with the olive oil and rub onto the inside surface of the roast, making sure to get some into all the cuts. Combine minced garlic with fennel fronds and parsley and spread over the surface. Tightly roll the roast and tie securely with kitchen string; rub the outside of the roast with reserved dry spice mixture. Wrap in parchment or waxed paper, place in a large (gallon-sized) zip-top bag, and refrigerate overnight.

2. Remove roast from refrigerator, unwrap, and place in a roasting pan or slow cooker, seam side down, fat side up; let come to room temperature. If roasting in an oven, preheat to 325 degrees; if roasting in a slow cooker, let meat rest for 30 to 45 minutes, then place on high. Slow roast for 4 hours in the oven or up to 6 hours in a slow cooker, until the meat shreds easily when pulled with a fork.

3. Serve warm or at room temperature on crusty, Italian hard rolls, with mustard and maybe a Peroni.

Cook's Notes: Placing the open roast on a rimmed baking sheet helps contain the inevitable mess when seasoning, rolling, and tying. Drying with paper towel before rubbing with the seasoning helps the meat draw in the spice mixture. Because porketta needs to roast at a low temperature for a long time, using a slow cooker is a great option; it helps tenderize the meat and hold the moisture in.

DAD'S DENVER SANDWICHES: UPDATED

[makes 4 big sandwiches]

At our house, ham on Sunday usually meant ham salad sandwiches in our lunch pails on Monday and split pea soup on Tuesday or Wednesday. If there was any left on Friday, Dad would usually hop in the kitchen around eight o'clock and whip up one of his special Denver sandwiches for a little nighttime snack to have while we watched the fights, or *The Twilight Zone*, or maybe an old movie on TV.

He'd cut up the leftover ham and some onion and green pepper, grab a couple of eggs and some milk, put everything in an empty canning jar, add some salt and pepper, put the lid on tight, and give it to my brother or me to shake as hard as we could. Then he'd melt some butter in the big cast-iron frying pan and put in as many slices of white bread as would fit at a time, lightly pan-toast them on one side, flip them over, and toast on the other side. I'd be in charge of lining them up on one of the big cutting boards that pulled out from under the counter.

When Dad had enough toasted bread slices, he'd put more butter in the pan, turn up the heat, give the eggs another good shake, and pour them in. Once they were light brown on the bottom, he'd flip them over, turn off the heat, and let the other side finish browning before sliding them out on the other big under-counter cutting board, where he'd cut them into triangular wedges and fit them onto half of the toasted bread slices. That was the signal for my brother or me to squirt ketchup out of the red squeeze bottle that had a little white drawing of a chef with a pointy mustache and floppy hat on the side. We took turns. If I didn't get to shake the eggs, I got to squirt the ketchup over the eggs on the toast. My brother would put the top piece on and Dad would cut the sandwiches into triangles, then we'd carry them on paper plates into the living room, where Mom had set up TV trays for us to use as tables.

It was simple; it was fun; it was delicious.

. . .

In this updated Denver, a dry Serrano-style ham takes the place of the water-injected version from the fifties, and mildly spicy poblanos stand in for the lackluster green bell peppers. A thickly sliced, dense egg bread like Challah (page 37) serves as a good absorbent foil against any of the new, spicy, pepper-based ketchups that are appearing on grocery store shelves; you get a round, toned-down flavor without the pain.

6 large eggs

3 tablespoons whole milk

½ cup finely chopped dry country ham (Serrano)

3 tablespoons finely chopped sweet yellow onion

¼ cup finely chopped poblano pepper

salt and freshly ground pepper

5–6 tablespoons salted butter

8 thick slices of good, moist egg bread (see head note)

hot and spicy tomato ketchup, your choice, if you dare

1. In a large bowl, combine eggs and milk; whisk until slightly frothy. Add ham, onion, and peppers; season with salt and pepper, and mix well.

2. Melt 1–2 tablespoons of the butter in a large skillet over moderate heat. Place as many slices of bread in the pan as will fit snugly. Watch carefully; when lightly browned, turn over and toast the other side. Repeat with remaining slices of bread, adding more butter as needed.

3. When all slices have been toasted, heat remaining butter in the skillet until foamy. Increase heat, vigorously whisk egg mixture, and quickly add to pan so it puffs up as it sets. Once the eggs have set, use a heatproof rubber spatula to turn eggs over, pressing down so they deflate. Remove from heat once eggs are lightly browned on the other side. Transfer to a cutting board and cut into 4 equal pieces.

4. Lay toasted bread slices on a cutting board, buttered side–up, and top 4 of them with a slice of cooked eggs. Spread spicy ketchup over eggs (if using), and top with remaining toast slices, buttered side–down. Secure with toothpicks at opposite corners if needed; slice diagonally with a good bread knife. Serve immediately.

Cook's Notes: *This sandwich is perfect for a late-night lunch, maybe with a cold bottle of Corona or Pacifica and a big wedge of lime.*

The Insides of Iron Miners' Lunch Pails

By the fifties, men's lunchboxes were standard issue for the most part: black metal, shaped like a barn, with two silver metal snap fasteners on the front. Inside, a white interior and a black, metal Thermos bottle—its red cup with a small looped handle covering a red stopper—cradled by the hump of the lid and held in place by a metal hinge that looked like a mini version of the bar one of the county fair carnies pulled across your lap on the Scrambler to secure you in your seat. Over time, the hinges and fasteners became loose, and something that looked like a giant safety pin would be slipped through the eye parts to keep the lid in place—not unlike repairs made to the work clothes the men wore.

• • •

Carmela Fiori, my friend and cooking teacher (see page 75 for her ravioli), gave me this list of names and lunch pail menus during a lesson in 2011, when she was ninety-two years old.

Blanche Carpenter, Hibbing
Husband Bob carried in his lunch pail
Meat sandwich (beef or pork roast, meatloaf, chicken) usually on white bread, sometimes home-made; homemade dill or sweet pickles; garden radishes, carrot sticks, and green onions in summer; store-bought celery and carrot sticks in winter; chocolate cake, always; a thermos of coffee; fruit— red delicious apples, home-canned peaches, pears, or plums, or store-bought fruit cocktail.

Lyn Minerich, Hibbing
Husband John carried in his lunch pail
Boiled beef salad with onions, salt and pepper, vinegar and oil; hardboiled eggs in vinegar and oil; pasties; meat sandwiches with pickled peppers; sliced dill pickles all the time; fresh or canned fruit all the time; a thermos of coffee.

Marge Bruno, Hibbing
Husband Louis Sr. carried in his lunch pail
Meat sandwiches every day; fresh fruit every day; fresh carrot and celery sticks every day; cake and a thermos of coffee.

Lou Strom, Hibbing
Husband L. A. carried in his lunch pail
Sandwiches with ham, pork, chicken, or egg salad; salad in a thermos; milk in a thermos and fruit.

CHAPTER 4

Suppers

Come you taste.
Is good.

ANNA CRNKOVICH
HIBBING, MINNESOTA, 1957

Suppers often included dishes that had either been prepared in quantity in advance and preserved or frozen, such as *Sarma* (page 88), Ravioli (page 75), or Lutefisk (page 79), and required minimal preparation before serving, or meals that had been started shortly after the midday dinner, like *Braciole* (pages 83), Crackling Roast Pork (page 92), or Swedish Meatballs (page 81), and slowly cooked over several hours.

Entire afternoons and weekends might be given over to making some of the more time-consuming recipes in big batches, with neighbors and family called in to help. The camaraderie was always welcome, and the extra hands made shorter work. On these occasions, favorite family recipes were shared and their making taught and passed on to the next generation. Though it may have seemed like work, these times were likely to be remembered with great fondness.

CARMELA'S RAVIOLI

[makes about 60 ravioli]

"This was the recipe my Grandmother Fiori brought from Italy, and Mom made it for many, many years. This quantity will make about sixty ravioli, and can be frozen. Wrap well." This advice comes from Jackie Fiori Hartnett of Bloomington, Minnesota, who grew up in Hibbing, where she learned how to make these ravioli from her mother, Carmela Fiori, who was given precise instructions by her mother-in-law.

. . .

Frozen, chopped spinach and freshly grated Parmesan give the ravioli filling a chewy texture and pronounced taste, but canned spinach combined with pre-grated Parmesan—in the green can—makes a smoother filling that is less likely to puncture a thinner pasta dough; breaking the ground beef into small bits while it's browning helps in this regard, too. Adding the seasonings to the beef while it's still warm will give you a more intensely flavored filling.

PASTA DOUGH

4 cups all-purpose flour

6 large eggs, plus 2 large egg whites

olive oil

FILLING

1 (15-ounce) can spinach, or 1 (10-ounce) box frozen chopped spinach, thawed

8 ounces lean ground beef

olive oil

salt

white pepper

garlic powder

nutmeg, freshly grated, optional

¼ cup grated Parmesan cheese (see head note)

1 large egg, beaten

1. To make the dough (see notes for alternative method), pour 3 cups of the flour into a high mound in the middle of a large work surface; set the remaining cup to the side. Make a well in the center of the flour with a spoon; be sure to leave flour at the bottom. Break the eggs directly into the well 1 at a time, beating with the tines of a fork and knocking a little flour into each egg as it is added; do this slowly so the flour wall doesn't collapse. Use the extra cup of flour to fortify the flour wall if necessary. Repeat until all 6 whole eggs have been added. Using the

>>

fork, gradually mix remaining flour into the beaten eggs; again, work slowly so the eggs don't break through the flour. Continue until all flour is incorporated into the eggs and the dough is too firm to mix with the fork.

2. Knead by hand, adding just enough flour to make a soft, sticky dough; brush excess flour to the side. Continue kneading for 5 to 10 minutes, until the dough is smooth and pliable, adding small amounts of flour as necessary; an impression should remain when you poke the dough with a finger. Shape into a round, place into a bowl with a few drops of olive oil, and turn to lightly coat. Tightly cover with plastic wrap and let sit for at least 30 minutes or several hours at room temperature; or refrigerate overnight and bring to room temperature before rolling.

3. To make the filling, drain spinach in a colander; press to force out as much water as possible. While spinach is draining, brown the ground beef over medium-high heat, with a little olive oil if needed, stirring to break into small bits. Stir seasonings—salt, pepper, garlic powder, nutmeg (if using)—into the warm ground beef and place in a large bowl to cool. Add drained spinach and Parmesan to the cooled, seasoned meat and mix by hand; add the beaten egg and mix well. Place a small amount of the filling in a small skillet and cook for about 1 minute; taste for seasoning and adjust if needed. Cover and refrigerate until cool, or overnight.

4. Before making the dough, scoop chilled filling into ¾-teaspoon-size portions onto a plate or baking sheet, cover, and refrigerate; chilled filling is easiest to handle when enclosing in pasta dough.

5. Assemble the ravioli. Lightly dust a work surface with flour. Beat the egg whites until frothy; set aside. Cut the dough into 6 slices, about 1 inch thick; flatten and shape into rectangles. Work with one piece at a time; cover the others with plastic wrap so they don't dry out.

6. Tightly clamp a pasta machine to the edge of the table or work surface, and set rollers on level 1 (see notes for alternative method). Feed the dough through the rollers twice, catching and holding the bottom edge as it comes out. Reset to level 3 and repeat. Reset to level 5 and repeat until the dough is in strips about 2 feet long and 3 inches wide; it should be shiny and elastic and easily handled without tearing.

continued on page 78 >>

Sons of Italy

*O*n Hibbing, if the names Vince, Leo, Jeno, or Sammy came up in conversation, everyone knew who, and what, was being talked about; last names didn't matter. All were sons of immigrants, all were successful food entrepreneurs, and all were Italian.

The Italians seemed to dominate local restaurant and neighborhood grocery endeavors, but these guys went above and beyond the small mom-and-pop corner store environs that several had been raised in, reaching regional and international stature. Vince Forti, Leo Fraboni, Jeno Paulucci, and Sammy Perella are quietly credited with bringing the Hibbing area to culinary prominence—though rightful commendation should go to their mothers and fathers, who nurtured their appreciation and value of food, teaching what they knew and setting their sons on paths of success.

Vince began his career at the Sunrise Bakery in 1938, alongside his father, who had founded it in 1913; Leo worked in his father's IGA in the early days of the Depression, leaving in 1968 to open his own off-shoot sausage and porketta business just up the street; Jeno worked with his mother in the small family grocery store during the Depression and opened his first food manufacturing business in Duluth in the forties; and Sammy left work in the mines to open his first pizza operation in 1953.

By 2015 their families had been in business both continuously and collectively for 334 years, growing from individual start-up businesses—that either they or their parents began—to international operations and philanthropic organizations. All endeavors are still very much alive, with over thirty restaurants, multiple wholesale and retail grocery operations in North Dakota, Minnesota, and Wisconsin complemented by extensive online presences, and several international philanthropic concerns. With the exception of Fraboni's, all are still family owned and operated by third- and fourth-generation descendants.

One other Hibbing-born son of Italian immigrants needs to be included on the list even though he grew up in California, where his family relocated when he was a very small child. His father was a good winemaker, having learned the trade from his father in Sassoferrato in the balmy Marche region of Italy on the Adriatic, which is why he moved his family to a more weather-hospitable situation. There he mentored his son in good life skills and practices, teaching him the crucial, fine points of viticulture and also engineering.

He established a successful fruit brokerage system, packing and shipping otherwise inaccessible produce, especially grapes for winemaking, to cooler regions outside of California. It was an enterprise that would become vitally important in feeding the nation and the world: his design and implementation of the first refrigerated boxcar system revolutionized the transportation of perishable foods year round to the most frigid areas of the country. Though the climate was kinder than the one they'd left behind in Minnesota, neither father nor son would forget their Iron Range roots.

When he was older, and on his way to great success as a winemaker, Robert Mondavi applied his viticulture prowess to his father's inventiveness,

>>

Sons of Italy *continued from previous page*

and in the late 1950s he established the California Wine House next to the railroad tracks on Hibbing's north end, just behind the Sunrise Bakery. For decades, refrigerated boxcar shipments of grapes from the Mondavi vineyards in California made their way to the trackside depot in northern Minnesota for use by the extensive community of Italian home winemakers, honoring Robert's roots and his father's life lessons.

7. Lightly dust 2 baking sheets with flour and set aside. Lay the strips of dough on the work surface and lightly brush half of the length with the beaten egg whites. Place evenly spaced portions of the chilled filling ¾ inch apart on the half brushed with egg white, with the final portion about half an inch from the edge of the dough. Carefully fold unbrushed half over the filling so all edges of dough are aligned; press the ends firmly together. Gently press down between each mound of filling with the side of your hand, then around each with your fingertips; try not to push into the filling. Seal and cut by running a ravioli cutter firmly along the length of the dough, then between each portion for square ravioli. Carefully separate ravioli with the tines of a fork, place on the floured sheet pans, and cover with plastic wrap. Repeat the process until all dough and filling have been used up.

8. Use the eye end of a large sewing needle to poke a small hole in the top of each ravioli to lessen the chance of it breaking open; if the hole is too big, water will seep in during cooking and cause the filling to leak out. Cover baking sheets with aluminum foil and freeze; once frozen, portion into zip-top bags or other freezable containers.

9. To cook, put ravioli into boiling salted water directly from the freezer, lower heat to medium so they don't break apart, and cook until pasta is tender; the timing will vary depending on the thickness of the dough. Pour into a colander or strainer to drain, shaking to remove excess water. Serve as desired.

Cook's Notes: *Making the dough in a food processor can be easier and faster, but you won't get as much of a tactile sense of when it is ready. Rolling out the dough by hand is harder; it takes a lot more experience to get it to an acceptable, even thinness. Top ravioli with your favorite sauce and freshly grated Parmesan cheese, or try Oven-Roasted Tomato Sauce (page 130).*

LUTEFISK

[serves 4]

"My mother used to buy her fish from Finland at the store over in Silica Location in late November; it was dried. First she would have to pull the skin off and any bones out. What a chore peeling that tough, dried skin off was! You didn't want to break those fish into pieces. Then she'd make some salted lye broth in one of her white enamel dishpans, lay the fish in and cover it with a dish towel that she'd tie on with string. She kept it in the little entry room shed just before you came into the kitchen, where it would sit maybe a week or more, and make it into lutefisk. Oh boy, did that smell strong when we'd come in from outside. We would cook it in the first part in December and have it with milk gravy and boiled potatoes and carrots from our garden. And she would have Swedish *Limpa* (page 20) that she had baked in our woodstove. The Norwegians said you were supposed to have it with hardtack (page 18) or lefse, but we liked our mother's homemade rye bread—it was sweet from the orange she put in—and some butter from our own cows to go with it. That was the best." Toward the end of her story, Linnea Eliason smiled and licked her lips slightly, almost as if she were tasting everything as she described it.

• • •

Lutefisk—translated from Norwegian as "lye fish"—is the white-sauced, North Atlantic–Baltic Sea milder version of the spicy tomato salt cod Yuletide dishes found in Italian (*baccalà*) and Spanish-Portuguese *(bacalao)* Mediterranean cuisines. Norwegians preserved their North Atlantic cod by hanging it, unsalted, from poles in outdoor drying sheds in the ideal weather of midwinter through early spring. It was kept cool and dry and reconstituted in a lye-based brine for serving in late fall into the winter, especially at Christmas, a practice replicated by their Swedish and Finnish neighbors on the Baltic Sea. Fast-forward from the twelfth century to the twenty-first, where home drying, peeling, and lye-solution soaking are no longer necessary, and enter Olsen Fish Company, the world's largest lutefisk producer, located right here in Minnesota. And it's the real deal. Olsen imports their *stockfish*—dried cod and other white fish—directly from Norway, processing it in the traditional method before packaging it to be sold as "kettle ready." Their lutefisk can be had year round in Scandinavian specialty shops and many grocery stores, especially late fall into early winter. In the right hands, this often-impugned dish traditionally served in the weeks leading up to Christmas can have an almost delicate elegance. Almost!

OLD-FASHIONED LUTEFISK

12 cups water	paprika, optional
1½ tablespoons sea or kosher salt	minced parsley, optional
2 pounds "kettle ready" lutefisk (see head note)	16 tablespoons (2 sticks) salted butter, melted, or white sauce (recipe follows)

1. Place water in a large saucepan and bring to a boil over high heat. Add salt, then fish. Cook for 8 to 10 minutes or until lutefisk flakes.

2. Carefully remove fish from water using a slotted spoon, pat dry with a cloth or paper towel, and place on a serving platter. Garnish top with a sprinkling of paprika and/or minced parsley (if using), and serve immediately with melted butter or white sauce.

OVEN LUTEFISK

2 pounds "kettle ready" lutefisk (see head note)	minced parsley, optional
1½ teaspoons sea or kosher salt	16 tablespoons (2 sticks) salted butter, melted, or white sauce (recipe follows)
paprika, optional	

1. Preheat oven to 375 degrees. Place lutefisk in a lightly buttered casserole dish, sprinkle with salt, and cover with aluminum foil. Bake 30 minutes or so, until lutefisk flakes.

2. Remove fish from pan to a platter; garnish with paprika and/or minced parsley (if using) and serve immediately with melted butter or white sauce.

Cook's Notes: *Lutefisk is traditionally served with boiled potatoes, buttered baby peas, and melted butter or a plain white sauce.*

WHITE SAUCE

4 tablespoons (½ stick) salted butter	2 cups whole milk, warmed
¼ cup all-purpose flour	½ teaspoon sea or kosher salt
	pinch white pepper

Melt butter in a small saucepan over medium heat. Stir in flour and cook for 2 to 3 minutes; the mixture should be thick but not brown. Whisk in warm milk; sprinkle in salt and pepper to taste. Remove from heat and keep warm until ready to serve.

VARIATIONS

For a more pronounced flavor, substitute ½ cup fish cooking water for ½ cup warm milk.

Add a pinch of ground allspice and/or 1 teaspoon dry mustard.

Cook a quarter to half a minced yellow onion in the butter before adding the flour.

SVENSKA KÖTTBULLAR / SWEDISH MEATBALLS

[makes 40–50 small meatballs]

Every culture seems to have a plump, signature meatball in its culinary portfolio, and most include a binder of rice or dried bread crumbs, many leaning toward the spicy side. Swedish meatballs—*svenska köttbullar*—distinguish themselves from all others for their petite size, tender texture, and sweet, creamy gravy, which may be the reason many Swedes refer to them as *Mamma's Köttbullar*—Mother's Meatballs.

• • •

To achieve the right texture and taste, a specific cooking method must be followed and, except for substituting ground turkey for the traditional ground veal, the ingredients need to remain the same: soft, fresh white bread crumbs, not dried; whole milk or cream, not low-fat; butter, not oil or margarine; and grated onion, not minced. A combination of lean and fatty ground meats is essential for flavor and texture, too. Beating—almost whipping—the ingredients in a specific order gives the meatballs their signature light, melt-in-the-mouth texture.

⅔ cup whole milk or half-and-half, warmed

4–5 slices soft white bread, crusts removed, cut into large pieces

>>

8 or more tablespoons unsalted butter, divided

1 large yellow onion, peeled and grated

½ pound ground pork

1 pound lean ground beef

1 pound ground veal or turkey

2 large eggs

2 teaspoons kosher salt

1 teaspoon finely ground allspice

1 teaspoon white pepper

½ cup all-purpose flour

3 cups beef stock, heated

½ cup sour cream

2–4 tablespoons lingonberry, red currant, or cranberry jelly, optional

1. Place the lukewarm milk in a large bowl, add the bread, stir, and let sit for 15 to 20 minutes. Once the bread has absorbed all the milk, vigorously beat with a wooden spoon until smooth. While the bread is soaking, melt 2 tablespoons butter in a large skillet over medium-high heat. Add grated onion to the butter, stir to coat, and cook until translucent, 3 to 4 minutes. Stir onions into the milk-bread mixture; set aside to cool.

2. Place ground meats in a bowl large enough to hold all ingredients and mix with your hands until well combined. In a separate bowl, beat eggs, add spices (salt through pepper), and beat until thick. Pour over ground meats and beat to loosen. Add soaked bread to meats in three parts, vigorously beating after each addition. This will produce the light, tender meatballs that are the hallmark of this dish.

3. Using two teaspoons dipped in water—one to measure; the other to scrape—scoop 1-inch portions onto a baking sheet. Once mixture is portioned, wet your hands and quickly round each into a smooth meatball—don't compress. Cover baking sheet and refrigerate for 15 minutes or more to firm up; this will help keep the tender meatballs from breaking apart during the browning.

4. Melt 6 tablespoons butter in a large skillet over medium heat. When the butter is foamy, reduce heat to medium low and brown meatballs in small batches so as not to crowd the pan. Carefully turn the meatballs to firm up and lightly brown on all sides; keep the heat low to medium so the butter doesn't become too brown or burnt. Once meatballs are set, remove to another pan and continue with remaining meatballs. The meatballs don't need to cook all the way through at this point; they'll finish cooking in the sauce.

5. After the meatballs are browned, there should be about 6 tablespoons of browned butter; add more if needed. If the butter has become too dark, discard it, wiping pan with paper towel, and replace with 6 tablespoons of fresh butter. Over medium heat, slowly whisk in the flour and stir until smooth. Continue stirring for several minutes, until the roux is light brown, the color of Swedish coffee with cream. Slowly stir the warm stock into the roux; reduce heat and return meatballs to the pan. Baste with the sauce, cover, and simmer over low heat for 10 minutes.

6. Using a slotted spoon, transfer the meatballs to a warmed serving dish. Stir the sour cream and jelly (if using) into the sauce, and pour over the meatballs.

Cook's Notes: *As an alternative to putting lingonberry jelly into the final gravy, consider making Lingonberry Sauce (page 53) and serving it on the side. Or gently warm the jelly and serve on the side if preferred.*

BRACIOLE / "COMPANY BEEF ROLLS"

[serves 6]

In early Iron Range homes, large quantities of meat—particularly prime cuts of steak—were considered luxuries, best reserved for special occasion dinners. Frugal Italian housewives would "fancy up" and extend inexpensive cuts of beef and pork by making *braciole* (pronounced *bra'zhul*). With these savory rolls of tenderized meat wrapped around bread crumbs, onion, and bits of ham, salami, or prosciutto, a mother could confidently feed both her large family and her company in style.

. . .

This recipe will generously serve six hungry people and goes well with Polenta (page 123). Before seasoning the flour, taste the prosciutto and cheese for saltiness. You will need a large counter or table surface to assemble these.

1 cup all-purpose flour seasoned
to taste with freshly ground
pepper and salt (see head note)

1½ pounds flank or boneless
round steak, sliced ½ inch thick

>>

6–9 thinly sliced pieces prosciutto or cured ham *(if you have or can afford)*

8 ounces mozzarella or provolone cheese, thinly sliced

1 cup fine, dried bread crumbs

¼ cup finely minced fresh parsley leaves, or 1 tablespoon dried

1 small yellow onion, finely minced

¼ cup grated Romano or Parmesan cheese, plus more for garnish

2 large hard-cooked eggs, finely chopped

1 large egg beaten with 1–2 teaspoons water

¼ cup good olive oil

4 cups Oven-Roasted Tomato Sauce (page 130)

12 medium or 18 small slices Polenta (page 123)

1. Lay 3 large sheets of plastic wrap on a counter or tabletop; sprinkle the surface of each with some of the seasoned flour mixture. Cut steak across the grain into 3 pieces and dry with paper towels. With the tip of a sharp paring knife, score meat surfaces in a crosshatch pattern and place each slice on a sheet of floured plastic wrap. Dust tops of steak with flour mixture, and cover each with a sheet of plastic wrap; set remaining flour mixture aside. Using a meat tenderizer or the bottom of a small, heavy pan, pound steaks into ¼ inch (or slightly less) thicknesses; peel top sheet of plastic away and turn each piece at least once.

2. Remove the top sheets of plastic and lay on work surface, floured sides up. Lay 5 pieces of kitchen string, cut in 12-inch lengths, across the width of each piece of plastic; place a slice of pounded steak over the strings, adjusting so strings are evenly spaced under each. Top each piece of steak with 2 to 3 slices of prosciutto or ham and 2 to 3 slices of mozzarella or provolone.

3. In a medium bowl, mix bread crumbs, parsley, onion, Romano or Parmesan, and hard-cooked egg. Stir in beaten eggs, adding a bit more water to bind the mixture if needed. Spread one-third of the mixture lengthwise down the middle of each slice of meat, leaving a one-inch margin on each end and a half-inch margin along each side.

4. Preheat oven to 325 degrees. While oven is heating, tightly roll each slice widthwise; position it seam side–down across the middle of the strings. Draw ends of string up around the meat and tie tightly at the top of each roll. Dredge rolls in reserved seasoned flour; set aside.

5. Pour olive oil into a heavy ovenproof pan large enough to hold all three rolls, and warm over medium heat. Place the rolls seam side–down in the hot oil and sear, turning so they brown evenly on all sides; adjust heat as needed. Top with red sauce, place in oven, and bake for 1 hour, basting with the sauce several times. Remove rolls to a platter or cutting surface with sides to catch juices, and cool until string can be removed.*

6. Brush a large, shallow casserole or 9 x 13–inch baking pan with olive oil; evenly spread half of the tomato sauce over the bottom of pan. Carefully cut and remove the strings from the rolls. Slice each roll at an angle into 1- to 1½-inch-thick pieces; place over tomato sauce in a single layer—slightly overlapped—and top with remaining sauce. Cover and bake for 45 to 60 minutes, until tender.

7. To serve, place 3 slices of *braciole* over warm slices of polenta and top with tomato sauce. Garnish with grated Romano or Parmesan cheese.

Cook's Notes: *Serve with greens like spinach, escarole, or chard sautéed in olive oil with thinly sliced garlic.*

*Braciole can be prepared a day ahead to this point: cover and cool in the tomato sauce overnight. Bring to room temperature before continuing.

JANSSON'S TEMPTATION

[serves 6]

In the old days, *Janssons Frestelse* (Temptation), a Swedish Christmas *smörgåsbord* tradition, was also a popular dish on midnight supper buffets through the depths of midwinter, filling guests with warm food and memories to carry on their journey home. The origin of the dish and its name is credited in various places, including having been concocted by Swedish opera singer and gourmand Pelle Janzon in the late 1880s, or being named by Swedish social matron Mrs. Stigmark for a dish prepared by her cook (Miss Jansson) and served at a society dinner. From whichever beginning, it spread to other households and found its way into the Swedish culinary lexicon. In time, early twentieth-century Swedish immigrants carried the dish and its Christmas tradition to the Iron Range, where it can be found on family tables and Lutheran church basement *smörgåsbords*.

• • •

Janssons Frestelse was originally made with pickled sprats, a common North Atlantic small forage fish. When sprats were nearly depleted by overfishing around the turn of the twentieth century, anchovies were substituted, and they stuck as the identifying flavor component. Brine-cured Swedish anchovies are a must for this dish. They're firmer, sweeter, and not as salty as the Italian variety and can be found in Scandinavian specialty shops and in most full-service grocery stores; look for a small red tin with the patriarchal image of King Oscar in ornamental military dress. If you can't find them, the Italian style will do, but drain and discard the oil. Russets are the potatoes called for in most recipes, but yellow-fleshed potatoes like Yukon Gold, Klondike, or Yellow Finn have a creamier texture with a deeper flavor and give the dish a more appealing appearance.

4 tablespoons (½ stick) unsalted butter, divided

2 large yellow onions, halved and sliced lengthwise to the root ¼ inch thick

1 pound (5–6) yellow flesh potatoes (see head note), peeled and sliced lengthwise ¼ inch thick

4–5 tablespoons unseasoned dried bread crumbs

1 (4–5 ounce) tin Swedish anchovy fillets, oil drained and reserved, fish chopped (see head note)

kosher salt and freshly ground pepper

1–1½ cups heavy cream, at room temperature

2–3 tablespoons fresh parsley, minced, optional

1. Preheat oven to 425 degrees. Melt 3 tablespoons of butter in a large skillet; pour 1 tablespoon melted butter into 2- to 3-quart casserole. Add sliced onions to skillet, stir to coat with remaining butter, and cook over medium heat until light brown; don't overcook.

2. While onions are cooking, place potato slices between several sheets of paper towels and blot dry. Brush melted butter over bottom and sides of the casserole.

3. Spread half of the bread crumbs over the bottom of the casserole; reserve remainder for topping. In evenly spread layers, top bread crumbs with half the onions, half the chopped anchovies, and half the potato slices. Season with salt and pepper. Repeat with remaining ingredients. Pour half of the heavy cream evenly over the mixture, and spread remaining bread crumbs over the top. Melt

remaining tablespoon of butter and combine with reserved anchovy oil; drizzle evenly over the bread crumbs.

4. Bake on the middle rack of the oven for 10 minutes. Pour remaining cream over top—just enough to come up to but not cover the bread crumbs. Lower heat to 300 degrees, and bake 20 to 30 minutes longer, until potatoes are tender (cream should be bubbling) and bread crumbs are nicely browned. Sprinkle with parsley if desired, and serve directly from the casserole.

GUBBEN RUNKA (OLD MAN ROCKING)

[serves 4–6]

"We moved from town to the farm in 1929 when I was nine years old, and the first thing I learned to cook from my mother when we got there was *gubben runka:* 'the old man in the rocking chair.' My mother was born in 1889 in Vora, Finland, where she learned it from her mother when she was a young girl. It's potatoes and onions and sardines, oil and all. During the Depression in the 1930s we ate this quite a little bit on the farm, with buttermilk we made from our own cows and hardtack we made ourselves too. A real tasty Finnish meal. I used the *sild* oil from the sardines and everything. And with the yellow potatoes that my brother Ewald grew, oh it's so good. Oh I liked that. When it was done cooking, you *smashed* it together! My mother would always make extra, and we would fry it up the next morning."

Linnea Eliason, age ninety-five, smiled at the memory. Unclasping the hands that had been quietly laying in her lap, she drew her arms up and apart, then brought her palms together in a thunderous clap just below her chin. "And oh, it tasted so good. *Ja, smokka brä gŭd!*"

● ● ●

Almost a poor-man's Jansson's Temptation (page 85), this Finnish version features sardines in *sild* in place of the drained anchovies found in its Swedish counterpart. Sardines are typically packed in *sild*, which comes from an extremely oily forage fish and can be strong in flavor. For a less fishy taste, try sardines packed in extra-virgin olive oil; the floral notes complement the buttery taste of the yellow flesh potatoes.

5 medium yellow flesh potatoes (Yukon Gold, Klondike, or Yellow Finn), peeled and chopped

1 medium yellow onion, coarsely chopped

1 (3.75-ounce) can sardines in *sild* or extra-virgin olive oil (see head note)

light cream, optional

1 tablespoon unsalted butter, plus more for serving

kosher salt

freshly ground pepper

1 small bunch parsley, minced, optional

1. Place 2 cups of water in a large pot and bring to a boil over high heat. Add a generous amount of salt to the boiling water, and add the potatoes and onion. The water should just barely cover the vegetables; remove any excess with a ladle. Cover the pot, reduce heat, and simmer for 15 minutes or until tender.

2. Drain oil from sardines and add to cooked potatoes. Do not drain the potatoes; they should have absorbed most of the water. If they're too wet, cook down with the cover removed; if too dry, add a little cream. Add sardines, butter, and salt and pepper to taste, and mash with a potato masher or the back of a large spoon. The mixture should be fairly smooth with bits of onion and flecks of sardine. Stir in minced parsley (if using).

Cook's Notes: *Serve with hardtack (page 18), butter, and Sliced Radish Salad (page 114). Refrigerate any leftovers, and in the morning shape into patties while the mixture is still cold. Heat 1 tablespoon unsalted butter with 1 teaspoon olive oil in a skillet until sizzling. Add potato patties, and fry over medium-high heat until crisp and brown on the bottom, then turn and brown other side. Delicious topped with poached eggs.*

SARMA / SLOVENIAN CABBAGE ROLLS

[serves 12 average or 6 very hungry people]

Always smiling, "Grandma Cabbage" was a neighborhood favorite who shared food and drink and the bounty of her garden. Her kitchen always smelled of yeasty bread and sauerkraut and what my mom called "pigs-in-the-blanket." Grandma Cabbage called them *sarma.*

• • •

Recipe adapted from *The Old Country Cookbook: Iron Range Ethnic Food*

1 large (3–4 pound) green cabbage, or 1 large sour-head*

1 cup uncooked long-grain white rice

1 pound ground beef

1 pound ground pork

1 medium yellow onion, finely chopped

1 large egg, beaten

½ teaspoon garlic powder

2 teaspoons kosher salt

1 teaspoon freshly ground pepper

2 pounds sauerkraut

6 smoked pork ribs, 1 large ham hock, or other smoked meat, optional

1 cup tomato juice or sauce

1 cup beef broth or water

*These whole heads of brined cabbage are ready to use, and they handle easier than fresh cabbage, eliminating the entire first step. If using, reduce the amount of salt by at least half. Sour-heads can be found in supermarkets and butcher shops on the Iron Range year-round and in the fall and winter months elsewhere. Cut the smaller leaves and pieces into thin ribbons and use in place of some of the sauerkraut called for in the recipe.

†Step can be done a day ahead.

1. Core the cabbage, removing as many of the thick ribs as possible. Immerse the whole cabbage head in salted, boiling water and cook until tender, so the leaves come away easily. Carefully drain so the head remains together, and refrigerate.† When the cabbage head is cool, carefully separate the leaves, cutting out any remaining large bits of rib. If using a sour-head, separate large leaves, reserving smaller ones and any pieces for use in the pot.

>>

Slovenian children in vegetable garden, Ely, Minnesota

2. While the cabbage leaves are cooling, place the rice and 2 cups of cold water into a large saucepan and bring to a rolling boil. Remove from heat, cover with a tight-fitting lid, and let sit for 10 minutes so rice will absorb the water. Uncover and drain any remaining liquid (the rice should be a bit hard to help bind the mixture together; it will finish cooking in the oven).*

*Step can be done a day ahead.

3. Combine the beef and pork with rice, onion, egg, garlic powder, salt, and pepper. Refrigerate for several hours or overnight. When chilled, scoop ⅓-cup portions onto a baking sheet. Wet your hands and mold each portion into a large egg-shaped oval; cover and refrigerate for 30 minutes or until firm.

4. Cover the kitchen table or countertop with clean dish towels. Lay out as many large cabbage leaves as you can fit on the towels; flatten each, taking care not to tear it. Place a portion of the meat mixture in the center of each leaf, fold the sides over the meat, and tightly roll into a bundle so the mixture stays inside; secure with toothpicks if necessary. Place seam side–down on a cookie sheet, loosely cover, and refrigerate for 30 minutes.

continued on page 92 >>

Sarma Tips

Ƨf you aren't able to find a sour-head, freezing the cabbage can make the leaves easier to handle than boiling a fresh head and removing the leaves.

A few days before you are planning to prepare the *sarma*, cut the core out of the cabbage, wrap the head in plastic, and place in the freezer. The day before making the *sarma* filling, remove the cabbage from the freezer, place in a bowl, and thaw overnight in the refrigerator; this softens the cabbage and makes the leaves easier to handle and fill.

The day you are making the *sarma*, remove the cabbage from its plastic wrap, place in a colander, and set in the sink to drain. Carefully pull away the large leaves a few at a time, shake off any excess water, and lay curved side–down on a cutting board. With a paring knife, make a V cut around the thick spine in the center of each leaf and remove. Stack leaves together in a bowl, repeating until only the small, center leaves of the cabbage head remain; reserve these to chop and add to sauerkraut in the baking dish.

At this point, assemble in the same way as when using a sour-head or boiled fresh cabbage.

Grandma Cabbage

Elderly women and widows around the Iron Range were often called "Grandma" by all the neighborhood children back in the 1940s, '50s, and '60s. One of my favorites was Grandma Crnkovich, a Croatian widow who lived on the corner of our block. She did all her own yard work, keeping the outside of her beige, stuccoed house as tidy as the inside. The sidewalks were always shoveled edge to edge in winter and swept in summer, and the front lawn mowed with precision, except in late April and early May, when the dark green grass was dotted with yellow dandelions. While some considered them weeds, she harvested the earliest, tender blossoms to make wine.

In the backyard she grew cabbage. Row after row of enormous, evenly spaced, blemish-free cabbage. No grass. No flowers. Just cabbage. Every day in summer she was outside, kneeling in her long skirt covered by an equally long apron, pulling weeds from around those giant, pale green globes. Her large, colorful scarf—loosely tied at the nape of her neck—and her wrinkled, sun-darkened skin were the perfect background for the heavy gold hoops dangling from her elongated earlobes. I thought she looked like an exotic gypsy.

She seldom spoke, and when she did her English was barely understandable, but she always had a shy, welcoming smile for the children on our block, who all loved her and had equal difficulty pronouncing her last name. To us she was "Grandma Cabbage." On hot summer days she'd beckon neighbor kids to join her grandchildren who'd come from down the street to run through

Grandma Ann Crnkovich watering her cabbages in her backyard garden in Hibbing

the sprinkler on her front lawn. She'd bring a tray of glasses filled with red Kool-Aid and a plate of large sugar cookies out on the front steps, inviting us all: "Come, you taste. Is good!"

Every fall Grandma Crnkovich shared her cabbage bounty with her neighbors, often sending one of the heavy heads home with me if she saw me playing in the alley. One September morning in the late 1950s she woke to find her immaculate garden destroyed; smashed cabbage heads littered the backyard and spilled out into the street. The *Hibbing Daily Tribune* wrote of it on the front page, calling it the destructive work of "juvenile delinquents," describing her quiet tears as she surveyed the ruins of her summer's labor. Family and neighbors, young and old, came to offer sympathy and help restore order in her backyard. She had no cabbages to share that year, but by the next summer row after row of perfect, round heads grew again, filling her backyard from the doorstep of the house to the garage at the alley.

That fall there were cabbages for everyone.

5. Preheat oven to 350 degrees. Line the bottom of a large ovenproof pot with sauerkraut or chopped sour-head and place the *sarmas* seam side–down on top; remove any toothpicks. Tuck smoked meat (if using) tightly between the *sarmas*. Add tomato juice and enough beef broth or water to cover. Bring to a boil, cover, and place in oven. Cook about 3 hours, adding more broth if needed.

6. Serve in shallow soup dishes or rimmed plates, topped with sauce from the pot.

Cook's Notes: *A fine accompaniment to* sarma *is good sour rye bread, sweet butter, and a cold, long-necked Pilsner. This recipe is easily doubled or tripled, and lends itself well to group participation. If making large quantities, layer only two* sarmas *deep in the pot; any more will make it difficult to remove them without breaking. Freeze in individual or multiple serving portions after cooking.*

CRACKLING ROAST PORK

[serves 6–8]

Many meat-eating cultures have signature pork dishes that are similar in taste and appearance, but the preparation method sets this Danish roast apart. With only two seasonings, this traditional special occasion dish is simple to make, but the resulting texture and flavor are anything but ordinary. Roasting the pork with the fat cap on in a very hot oven over boiling water is the key to a delectable, crispy exterior, and the floral notes of the bay laurel put it over the top.

• • •

Select a bone-in pork loin roast that has a heavy fat cap, or rind; do not trim. Have the butcher remove the backbone, but leave rib bones in place to make carving a snap. Meats should always be at room temperature before going into the oven, and ovens should be preheated to the correct roasting temperature. Drying the outside of the roast before salting and inserting the bay leaves, and roasting at a high heat will give you a crispier outside texture.

1 (5-pound) bone-in pork loin roast with a heavy fat cap

1–2 tablespoons kosher or coarse sea salt

10–12 bay leaves (choose the long, thin California laurel type)

1. Preheat oven to 450 degrees; position rack in the center. Dry the roast with paper towels. Use the tip of a sharp paring knife to score the fat cap in ½-inch-deep incisions that are ½ inch apart lengthwise and 1½ to 2 inches apart crosswise. Rub the exterior of the roast with the salt, and tuck the bay leaves into the incisions.

2. Put the roast—fat cap up—on a wire rack inside a roasting pan, place in the preheated oven, and roast for 30 minutes. Bring 4 cups water to a boil. Pour the boiling water into the roasting pan, reduce the heat to 400 degrees, and continue roasting until the internal temperature reaches 160 degrees when tested with an instant-read thermometer, about an hour. Keep an eye on the water, and add more boiling water if needed.

3. After removing the roast from the oven, immediately cut off the crackling fat cap and set aside in a dish; let the roast rest on the rack for 10 minutes before carving.

Cook's Notes: *Serve thinly sliced with the crackling rind, Sugar-Browned Potatoes (page 126), and glazed baby carrots.*

CHAPTER 5

Starters, Salads, Soups, & Sides

Antipasto—Parboil all vegetables (using 1 qt. measures) . . . Cost about 10.⁰⁰ (that was in 1970)

MARY SPADACCINI JACOBSON
HIBBING, MINNESOTA, AUGUST 1978

*E*ven in the leanest of times, most Iron Range tables had two or three small dishes to complement the main item, no matter how modest. Jams, cheese, and jellies at breakfast; soups, crackers, and something pickled at midday dinner; salads, potatoes, pasta, or other starches, and some form of vegetable at supper; and sweets without exception. All these culinary accessories were largely interchangeable, dependent on availability of time, funds, and ingredients. And through years of neighborly exchange, many continue to appear as a cross-cultural *smörgåsbord* at Iron Range picnics and celebrations.

CARMELA'S PICKLED PEPPERS

[makes 4 pints]

In the early part of the present century, I had the good fortune to do some canning with Carmela Fiori, a feisty little nonagenarian Italian who kept the fruit room beneath the steps of her back door in the Brooklyn area of Hibbing filled with jars of antipasto, tomatoes, and these pickled peppers, one of her standards. She made multiple batches every fall and always had one or two open in her refrigerator to eat straight from the jar, in chopped salads, or on porketta sandwiches (page 68) made from one of her down-the-street neighbor Leo Fraboni's roasts. This scaled-down version of her recipe uses one pound of peppers instead of two bushels. Wide-mouth pint canning jars are the easiest to pack; make sure to cut the pepper strips the same length and size so they stay in place.

1 pound (about 10) peppers: yellow banana, green bell, red bell, halved lengthwise, seeds removed

hot pepper flakes, optional

8 large garlic cloves, halved

3 cups distilled white vinegar (5 percent acidity)

2 cups filtered or distilled water

2 tablespoons kosher or pickling salt

pinch sugar

1. Slice pepper halves into half-inch strips, trim rounded ends so strips are flat and the same height as pint canning jars. Tightly pack into jars so they stand up and won't float. If adding red pepper flakes, press on garlic halves. Tuck garlic between pepper slices, 4 pieces per jar.

2. In a small saucepan, heat vinegar, water, salt, and sugar, stirring to dissolve salt and sugar. Cool to room temperature. Pour over peppers, covering completely. Screw on lid and refrigerate for 2 days before eating. Peppers will keep in the refrigerator for up to 3 months.

Antipasto
Parboil all vegetables
(using 1 qt. measures)

Pole Beans, button onions,
celery, carrots, 8 med cukes,
green peppers, cauliflower (2 med)
3 qts. olives (dark + green)
5 cans Tuna (Tonno brand)
1 qt. mushrooms

Boil about 1 Hr.
1 qt. mazola oil
1 qt. white vinegar
1 qt. chopped Parsely
1 qt. strained tomatoes
1 Bottle Ketsup (143)
½ lb. Anchovies
1 clove garlic (remove later)
red pepper (optional)

add the above vegetables to
liquid mixture, bring to
a boil + then add olives
add Tuna + olives
when thoroughly hot over

Beat in hot jars +
steam about 15-20 min.
Makes 20 pints.

Buying ingredients for Antipasto
4 large or 8 med peppers (green + red)
2 lbs button onions
(as) buy in bottles (1)
2 (one lb. jars Black olives (2 sizes)
green + stuffed olives
13 g can anchovies
4-5 (4 oz cans button mushroom
do not use whole button "
Cost about 10.00 (that was in 1970)

P.S. 8-24-78 Mom
Be sure the bottles are
wiped dry before the
sealing lids put on

ANTIPASTO

[makes 20 pints]

Antipasto—Parboil all vegetables (using 1 qt. measures) . . .
Cost about 10⁰⁰ (that was in 1970) Mom 8-24-78
P.S. Be sure the bottles are wiped dry before the sealing lids are put on.

So read the notes at the top and bottom of the olive oil– and tomato-stained recipe written on yellowing sheets of paper from a promotional tablet advertising a St. Paul fabrication company. "Mom" was Mary Spadaccini Jacobson of Hibbing, and the 1970 ten-dollar cost was for a single batch—twenty pints—of her antipasto, a price that wouldn't cover the jars and lids in today's world, let alone the ingredients. Oh, how times have changed.

During canning season—which coincided with the hot, humid days of late August and early September—Mary could always be found at a card table and small four-burner gas stove in the cool confines of the basement making antipasto. And down in the basement those pints jars would stay, until just before Christmas, when they became gifts for family and friends. No amount of wheedling or cajoling by anyone, including immediate family members, could get Mary to bend her policy; antipasto did not appear on her own table until Christmas Eve.

She was very specific about the type of mushrooms and tuna to be used: button mushrooms—canned and sliced, not whole; and Italian tuna packed in olive oil. Sure, it cost more, but she insisted it was the best. I increased the amount of tuna in her recipe from five cans to six or even seven. Within the last decade the commercial fishing industry has reduced the standard can sizes of tuna from six ounces to five.

When her daughter Cathi shared this recipe with me, she pointed out the curious amount of garlic her mother––a full-blooded, first-generation Italian— specified for the entire twenty-pint batch—*1 clove garlic (remove later)*—which gave us both a good laugh. I bumped it up to ten large cloves cut in half and cooked with the liquid to capture the full garlic flavor. You just might want to leave them whole—or even add more.

· · ·

There are quite a few steps involved in making antipasto, a number of which need to be taken care of before preparation and cooking can begin. I enlist two or three friends, and we break it into a two- to three-day schedule, several hours each day. The first: shopping, generally the farmers market, followed by a trip to an Italian specialty shop or a grocery store for canning supplies and any non-produce food items. The second: prepping vegetables; clearing counter spaces; setting everything out in the areas and order they'll be used. The third: getting down to business. With three or more people, and dividing the shopping and prepping duties, making it in two days is very manageable. Having more than one canning kettle makes the processing go faster, too. Included are a sidebar on blanching the vegetables in preparation for canning and instructions for processing in a hot water bath. I recommend reading them through once before setting up your work stations and ingredients, then a second time before beginning each procedure.

Yes, it is pricey; yes, it is labor intensive—but both fade next to the tasty results and the high praises you'll receive from family and friends, especially if you make them wait until Christmas.

4 cups Italian pole beans, cut in 1-inch pieces

4 cups carrots, peeled and cut in 1-inch pieces

4 large or 8 medium green and red peppers, cores and seeds removed, cut in 1-inch pieces

2 medium heads cauliflower, cut in 1-inch florets

4 cups celery, cut in half-inch pieces

8 medium cucumbers, not too thick, skin on and cut in 1-inch pieces

4 cups corn oil

4 cups distilled white vinegar

4 cups canned plum tomatoes, strained

1 (14-ounce) bottle ketchup

8 ounces anchovies packed in olive oil

10 large cloves garlic, halved

6–7 (5-ounce) cans Italian tuna packed in olive oil, undrained

2 pounds pearl onions bottled in vinegar, undrained

2 (16-ounce) jars whole pitted black olives

2 (16-ounce) jars stuffed green olives

4 cups loosely packed chopped Italian parsley leaves

4–5 (4-ounce) cans sliced button mushrooms

1. Blanch the prepared vegetables following the recommended guidelines in the sidebar on page 101.

2. In a large, heavy-bottomed saucepan, combine oil, vinegar, tomatoes, ketchup, anchovies, and garlic. Place over high heat, and bring to a slow boil for 45 minutes, stirring occasionally to keep from scorching; elevate by placing a second burner grate under the pot if necessary.

3. While the liquid is cooking, prepare 20 canning jars, lids, and rings according to the manufacturers' recommendations; also see processing sidebar on page 102. Remove the rack from the canning kettle, fill three-fourths full of water, cover, and place on burner to start heating.

4. After 45 minutes, add blanched vegetables to the saucepan, stir to combine, and bring to a boil. Add tuna, onions, olives, parsley, and mushrooms, gently stir, and cook until mixture is thoroughly hot but not boiling.

5. Bring water in canning kettle to a boil, and fill a large pot or teakettle with water and bring to a simmer. Use a large-mouthed canning funnel to fill warm jars with antipasto—about 2 cups—just up to the bottom of the jar neck; don't

pack in too tightly, and leave headroom for expansion. Wipe rims with a clean hot cloth, top with warm lids, and secure with rings; don't over tighten: there needs to be a small space for the rubber ring to expand and seal as it heats.

6. Put lidded jars in the canner rack and slowly lower into the boiling water. There should be enough water to completely submerge the jars; if not, add some hot water from the teakettle. Cover and bring to a boil for 15 to 20 minutes. Turn off heat, remove the lid, and carefully lift the rack out of the water and securely hook on the sides of the kettle or lower into a sink. Use a jar lifter to take bottles out of the rack and place on a cooling rack so the air can circulate underneath. Listen for the jar lids to pop as they seal. Test by tapping on the center of each lid; it should produce a dull sound. If it sounds hollow, the seal hasn't set. Return jars to the boiling water bath for an additional 5 minutes; remove and retest.

7. Store jars in a cool, dark place, and let the antipasto cure for at least 1 month before opening.

Cook's Notes: *Serve as an appetizer, with crostini or thin slices of Italian bread, hard cheese, and a dry Italian red wine. Given the large number of ingredients, this recipe makes a lot, but it's a great gift, especially around the holidays.*

Blanching Antipasto Vegetables

Blanching times are in minutes, based on the sizes of specific vegetables. The amounts listed are the equivalent of 2 measured cups, or 1 pint in volume, blanched in 4 cups of water.

VEGETABLE	SIZE	QUANTITY	TIME (MINUTES)
Carrots	1 inch	1–1½ pounds	2
Cauliflower	1- or 2-inch florets	1¼–1½ pounds	2–3
Celery	½ inch	¾–1 pound	3
Cucumbers	1 inch	2–3 pounds	1–1½
Italian pole beans	1 inch	2–4 pounds	2–4
Peppers	1 inch	1–1½ pounds	1–1½

Vegetable Blanching Basics

EQUIPMENT

1 or 2 large (6- to 8-quart) cooking pots

several large bowls

several bags of ice

1 or 2 long-handled strainers

large colander

long-handled slotted spoon

long tongs

large terrycloth and/or paper towels

several sets of hot pads, with spares in case they get wet

plenty of open counter space on either side of the stove and sink

a reliable kitchen timer

cutting board

SET-UP AND PROCEDURE

Set out equipment and tools in the areas you'll be using them.

Rinse and peel or trim all vegetables; cut to desired sizes and set aside until ready to proceed. Each variety should be blanched separately.

Place 4 quarts of *unsalted* cold water in a pot and bring to a rapid boil. While water is heating, spread terrycloth towel on counter next to sink; set colander in sink. Set up ice water bath(s) in a large bowl: 1 part ice to 1 part water. Place on towel.

Plunge vegetables in 1-pound batches into the rapidly boiling water and immediately begin timing; blanch for specified time listed on page 101.

Use strainer to quickly remove vegetables to the ice water bath to stop the cooking; stir with slotted spoon to ensure fast, even cooling. Let sit for several minutes; replace ice as needed.

Remove to colander with strainer or slotted spoon and shake to remove excess water. Place in containers until ready to use.

STUFFED ARTICHOKES À LA CARMELA

[serves 4]

Artichokes: these exotic globes were hard to come by in northern Minnesota in the first half of the twentieth century. There would have to be a thoughtful visitor from California in town for them to appear. When they did become available, it was largely through the efforts of a former Iron Range Italian immigrant, Cesare Mondavi, who re-transplanted his family to northern California in the 1920s. He's credited with pioneering the refrigerated boxcar system that made delivery of fresh produce possible across the country. His son, Bob, who was born in Hibbing, made quite a name for himself, too. When he grew up, he became one of California's first commercial grape growers and winemakers. You might've heard of him.

2 large artichokes, firm with tight leaves

1 lemon, halved

1½ cups (2–3 slices) day-old Italian bread, torn into small pieces

½ cup (2 ounces) freshly grated Romano or Parmesan cheese or a combination

2 tablespoons olive oil, plus more for brushing leaves

4 cloves garlic, smashed and minced

2 tablespoons chopped fresh Italian parsley leaves

sea or kosher salt and freshly ground pepper

¼ cup chicken or vegetable broth

melted butter mixed with some extra-virgin olive oil, for brushing and dipping

1. Heat oven to 400 degrees. With a serrated knife, slice off the top third of each artichoke; discard tops. Scoop out and discard the fuzzy choke. Spread artichoke petals open as far as possible without snapping; quickly rinse under cold, running water. Hold by stem and shake excess water into sink. Cut stems off so bottom is level and artichoke can stand up on its own without tipping over. Rub top edges and bottom with lemon halves; place artichokes cut side–down in a colander and set in sink to drain. Set aside lemon halves.

2. In a food processor, quickly pulse bread pieces into pea-size crumbs; don't overprocess. You should have about 1½ cups. Transfer to a medium bowl and

>>

toss with Romano or Parmesan, olive oil, garlic, parsley, juice from one lemon half, salt, and pepper. Taste and adjust seasonings as needed.

3. Set one artichoke on a plate or in a small pan, right side–up; spread leaves open as much as possible without tearing or breaking. With a teaspoon, evenly distribute half of the filling between open leaves of artichoke; reshape artichoke by pushing leaves back in place. Repeat with second artichoke.

4. Pour broth in bottom of a small glass or ceramic baking dish; snuggle artichokes in close together. Fill in any extra space with folded parchment or aluminum foil to keep artichokes upright while baking. Brush tops with olive oil and butter; tightly cover entire dish with aluminum foil. Bake for 40 to 50 minutes or until tender at the base; test with the tip of a sharp knife or a metal skewer. Unwrap, and continue baking until crumbs are toasted and golden brown, 5 to 7 minutes longer.

5. Serve on individual plates—one placed between two people—with a small dish of olive oil and butter, pieces of lemon from the remaining reserved half, and a dish to discard artichoke leaves.

Cook's Notes: *Artichokes are available in midwinter; this is a great appetizer to serve for Valentine's Day or another romantic occasion. Spice 'em up with red pepper flakes in place of the ground pepper. The olive oil–butter and lemon combo makes them finger-lickin' good; but if you're shy, have some wet towelettes at hand.*

JUUSTOLEIPÄ / FINNISH "SQUEAKY" CHEESE

[makes 1 big cheese]

This raw-milk Finnish cheese—a dairy farm standard through the mid-twentieth century that became overlooked in the last half as "too much work"—is enjoying a popular resurgence. Although it was traditionally broiled to color the surface, frying it in a little oil gives a more golden-brown, rind-like quality to the outside and adds a slight rich tone to this otherwise mild, clean-flavored farmstead cheese.

Linnea Eliason, age ninety-five, shared this memory: "In summer my mother would make rennet cheese with the milk from our 'Lil Un' [referring to a calf using a colloquial Swedish term of affection for a small child] that she would bake then fry, and we always called it squeaky cheese because when you bit into it, you squeaked like a mouse!"

. . .

Rennet, which produces the curd that gives solid form to cheese, is an enzyme taken from the fourth stomach of unweaned calves. It can be found in co-ops and health food and brewing supply stores. If none of these are an option, most grocery stores carry Junket rennet tablets; you may need to increase, even double, the amount called for in a recipe when using this type.

2 gallons whole milk (unhomogenized is best)	2 tablespoons iodized or canning salt
3 tablespoons white sugar	1 teaspoon liquid rennet, or 1 equivalent-size rennet tablet crushed into 1 tablespoon cool water (see head note)
3 tablespoons cornstarch	

1. In a large, heavy-bottomed saucepan, heat milk to 88 degrees; don't exceed 90 degrees, and don't scald. Remove from heat and stir in sugar, cornstarch, salt, and rennet. Cover with a loose-fitting lid or a cotton dish towel and set aside—away from any draft—until set, between 1½ and 2 hours, depending on the type of rennet and the room temperature. Test by inserting the handle of a wooden spoon into the curd; when properly jelled, the spoon will leave behind a clean hole. The texture should be jelly-like and not curdled and should slide away from the sides of the pot when you shake it.

2. Once it has set, use a large stainless steel spoon to cut through the mixture until it has a cottage cheese–like consistency. Cover and allow to settle for 20 to 30 minutes, until the mixtures melds together at the bottom of the pot. Preheat oven to 400 degrees. Line a colander or fine-mesh sieve with cheesecloth and set over a bowl or pot. Carefully pour the curd into the colander, pull the cheesecloth over the curd, and press down to force the whey out; reserve whey for other uses (see notes).

3. Press the curd into a 9 x 13–inch glass or stainless steel pan and bake in the preheated oven for 10 minutes; remove, press and drain whey, turn over in pan,

>>

and return to oven for 5 minutes. Remove from oven and place under a broiler until lightly browned on top; turn, drain any residual whey, and place under broiler to brown; remove from pan to a cooling rack to dry for several hours. Cut into smaller pieces or wedges if desired; wrap with waxed paper and plastic wrap and refrigerate.

Cook's Notes: This cheese can be eaten alone; with a bit of ham or smoked salmon and sliced dill pickles; or topped with strawberry jam and brown sugar and warmed in the oven—a favorite with kids of all ages. Before pressing the curd, mix in minced jalapeños or diced yellow onions browned in butter, or add a bit of eggnog when mixing in the rennet for a Squeaky Yuletide Cheese. Because nothing was wasted, the whey was used in breads, pancakes, puddings, and cakes, or given to the barn cats as a reward for keeping the field mice population out in the field.

BEDET EINGEMACHTS / JEWISH BEET PRESERVES

[makes 4–5 pints]

"I can remember my grandparents putting a tablespoon of this recipe in a glass of hot tea."
RUTH BRIZER

Beets—like rutabagas—are another cold-climate root that gets a bad rap. Well, I'm here to tell ya, these beet preserves are utter ambrosia, and, yes, a bit in a cup of hot tea *is* lovely. This is an adapted version of a recipe "passed down for generations among Jewish families" and contributed by Ruth Brizer to the 2004 edition of *The Old Country Cookbook: Iron Range Ethnic Food,* published cooperatively by Iron World Discovery Center and WDSE television in Duluth.

. . .

This recipe relies on the juice from the beets and lemons for its cooking liquid. Beets by themselves have a high sugar content and must be carefully watched when cooked slowly with additional sugar, as in this recipe. Finely dicing the beets and lemons will help draw out the maximum amount of their juice. I recommend using a simmer ring or a flame tamer, one suitable for both gas and electric burners. These inexpensive tools are available in most hardware or specialty cooking stores. If you've never tried one, you'll be amazed at what a useful device this is for cooking things slowly over an extended period of time, especially when using electric burners, which are harder to regulate.

These preserves are very sweet. You can increase the amount of ginger and lemon if you want a little more heat and tartness, or you can cut back on the sugar—but not too much, or the preserves won't thicken properly. Try making a full recipe first, then adjust the ingredients to taste for the next batch. And, trust me: you *will* be making a next batch.

2 pounds beets	1 tablespoon ground ginger
3 lemons	1 cup almonds
4½ cups white sugar	

1. Peel beets, rinse with cold water, and cut into quarter- to half-inch pieces. Place in a deep, heavy-bottomed saucepan. Scrub lemons and cut into thin—quarter-inch or less—slices; remove any seeds. Add to saucepan, along with any juice from the cutting board.

2. Mix together sugar and ginger in a large bowl. Coarsely chop almonds into tiny pieces; stir into sugar and ginger, and add to beets and lemon. Mix very well, stirring in all sugar from inside edge of the pan.

3. Cook over low to moderate heat for 1 hour; stir several times to keep from scorching on the bottom of the pan, especially along the inside edge (see head note).

4. Remove from heat when beets and lemon have broken down and mixture is thick. Pour into sterilized pint-size jelly jars and cover with lids and rings; place on a rack until cool. Tighten lids, and store in a cool, dark place to retain the bright color; refrigerate after opening. Or use a clean crock with a lid; cool to room temperature and then refrigerate.

Cook's Notes: *These preserves look especially beautiful in embossed jelly jars and would make a lovely gift with Ginger-Rhubarb Scones (page 13) or a braided loaf of Finnish Biscuit (page 31).*

JEWISH CHOPPED LIVER

[makes 1 small (3-cup) crock]

There are a few slight variations in making chopped liver; most are a matter of taste and ingredient availability. The liver can be chicken, beef, or calf—individually or in combination; fresh if you can find it. Sometimes shortening or oil is substituted for the traditional *schmaltz*—rendered chicken fat—if none is available or for health reasons, though some say *schmaltz* is the only fat that should be used. The rendered fat gives the chopped liver its true flavor, and inclusion of the chopped *grebenes* (cracklings)—the crisp chicken skin remaining after the fat has been rendered—gives it its traditional texture. Be sure to keep out some *schmaltz* for cooking the liver, and some to pour over the top for a seal in the refrigerator; warm to room temperature and stir in before serving.

. . .

Combining the mixture with the salt while both the liver and the eggs are still warm will greatly enhance the flavor. Serve it spread on hardtack (page 18) or pieces of thinly sliced *Limpa* (page 20) or as a dip for celery hearts. It's a great side with Sliced Radish Salad (page 114). Note that the method calls for a food processor or a meat grinder.

3 large eggs

1 pound good fresh liver, chicken, calf, beef, or a combination

1 large yellow onion, grated

salt and black pepper

2 tablespoons *schmaltz* (rendered chicken fat; recipe follows), oil, or shortening, plus more for frying liver and some to seal for storage

chicken cracklings (recipe follows), optional

1. Place eggs in a small saucepan, cover with cold water, and bring to a boil over high heat. When the water comes to a boil, immediately remove pan from the heat, cover, and let sit for 12 minutes. Drain eggs, cool slightly, and remove shells; place in a bowl, cover with a dish towel, and set aside.

2. While eggs are resting, cook the liver by your preferred method: frying in a bit of *schmaltz*, oil, or shortening, simmering in a little water to cover, or broiling,

until just firm to the touch; the liver should be tender and moist, still pink on the inside. Place cooked liver in a large dish or the bowl of a food processor; if the liver is large, cut into smaller pieces before putting in the processor bowl.

3. If liver was fried, add grated onion to the pan (or heat a bit of fat in a skillet, then add onion); cook until slightly brown, 1–2 minutes. (Onion may be used raw.) Add to cooked livers. Sprinkle with salt and pepper to taste.

4. Roughly chop warm eggs and add to cooked liver and onion; add *schmaltz*, shortening, or oil and cracklings (if using). Process by pulsing until all ingredients have broken down, then scrape the sides of the bowl and process until smooth. If using a meat grinder, toss ingredients together in the bowl and feed into the hopper—fitted with a medium-fine plate—and push through with a plunger while turning the blade. Taste; adjust seasonings as needed. To store, place in container slightly larger than the amount of chopped liver you have; smooth the surface, top with a film of the reserved *schmaltz* (see head note), cover with plastic wrap, and refrigerate for up to 1 week.

Cook's Notes: *The above method produces perfect hard-boiled eggs. Pushing the eggs through a ricer and tossing with finely minced parsley, then adding the egg-parsley mixture to the liver and onion after they've been ground will bring a bit of color to the otherwise gray-brown dish. Reserve some of the egg-parsley mixture and use as a garnish for chopped liver spread on hardtack; add a thin slice or two of radish or minced celery heart and a few grinds of black pepper for further texture and color.*

SCHMALTZ AND GREBENES

breast and thigh skin from 1 chicken	1–2 tablespoons cold water
1 pound chicken fat, cut or stripped from chicken	1 medium yellow onion, finely chopped

1. Rinse chicken skin and fat, removing any blood; cut in small pieces. Put in a heavy-bottomed saucepan with water; simmer over very low heat until all water has evaporated, fat has rendered, and skin pieces are crisp and brown.

>>

2. Add chopped onion; simmer until light brown. Strain fat into a glass bowl or container; refrigerate or freeze if not using right away. Remove cracklings, chop, and add to recipes or sprinkle over salad.

SCANDINAVIAN LIVER PASTE

[serves 10 or more as an appetizer or 4–6 in sandwiches]

This spiced spread is found on every Scandinavian buffet table, next to the hard-tack and traditional *smörgåsbord* toppings. Called a paste, it's really a baked loaf that is served sliced for sandwiches. Its creamy texture is spreadable, making it the perfect open-faced sandwich anchor for sliced radishes, beets, celery, or hard-cooked eggs. Make it several days ahead of when you plan to serve it; the flavors will be blended and the loaf easier to slice or spread.

. . .

Unlike its Jewish counterpart, this spread is made only from tender calf's liver; beef liver is too strong in flavor and, like chicken liver, too veined and coarse in texture. Fresh liver is ideal but not always easy to find; check with your local butcher for availability. This recipe is best made using a grinder attachment for a stand mixer or a traditional table-clamp meat grinder. A food processor can be used; be sure to grind and pulse the mixture until it is as smooth as possible. Partially freezing the liver makes it easier to force through the fine blade of the meat grinder. Use the freshest ginger and white pepper you can, and don't be afraid of the anchovy: it's only a seasoning, but a very important one.

5–6 pieces thinly sliced bacon

1 pound fresh calf's liver, slightly frozen

2 tablespoons unsalted butter

1 small yellow onion, grated

2 large eggs

2 teaspoons fine sea salt

2 tablespoons brandy

1 cup light cream or half-and-half

¼ cup unseasoned bread crumbs, finely crushed

1 teaspoon white sugar

1 teaspoon ground ginger

½ teaspoon finely ground white pepper

2–3 tablespoons anchovy paste

1. Line a 5 x 9–inch loaf pan with strips of bacon; all surfaces should be covered, with ends hanging over the sides. Preheat oven to 350 degrees and bring a kettle of water to boiling. Using a meat grinder fitted with the fine blade, push the partially frozen liver through the grinder into a large bowl (see head note). Melt the butter in a small pan, add grated onion, and cook over medium heat until light brown. Add to ground liver; mix well.

2. In a medium bowl, beat the eggs with the salt and brandy, add cream and bread crumbs; beat to combine. In a separate small bowl, mix together sugar, ginger, and pepper; add anchovy paste, and mix well. Combine seasonings with egg mixture and add to ground liver. Using a wooden spoon, beat until mixture becomes light and slightly fluffy. Pour into prepared loaf pan, smoothing the surface with a rubber spatula; fold ends of bacon over the top. Cover with a piece of parchment or waxed paper large enough to overlap the sides; use kitchen string to tie securely in place.

3. Place larger pan with rack or trivet in the bottom in the oven (see notes); place the loaf pan on the rack; pour in enough hot water around the loaf pan to reach almost the top. Bake for 1½ hours. Remove entire setup from oven to a rack; cool to room temperature in the water bath with the paper still tied around the pan. Remove and wipe all water from sides and top of the loaf pan, and refrigerate. The bacon-wrapped paste will keep for 2 weeks; seal tightly in plastic. Once unwrapped, use within a week.

4. To serve: remove parchment or waxed paper, peel back bacon, and turn loaf out onto a platter; remove and discard strips of bacon. For sandwiches, slice with a thin-bladed knife that has been run under hot water; as a spread, garnish around the base with some minced parsley or red onion, capers, finely chopped hard-cooked egg, or a combination of these.

Cook's Notes: The mixture needs to be steamed like an oven pudding and not browned on the surface like a traditional meatloaf. An ovenproof glass loaf pan works very well here, and a roaster is perfect for the water bath.

SILLSALAT / CREAMED HERRING SALAD

[serves 5–6]

Herring is the team player of salad fish, working well in combination with other ingredients. Swedes and Finns made versions of this salad, sometimes using up bits and pieces of vegetables they had on hand; other times making their specific interpretation—or, like this one, possibly a little of both. More than a salad, with all the additions it becomes practically a full meal in itself. It's perfect for picnics or lunch in the evening, and makes a beautiful presentation surrounded by baby lettuces, with some Finnish Hardtack (page 18) or Swedish Rusks (page 15) on the side.

Pickled herring keeps indefinitely, so lay in a store that you can dress up for the party and call it your own. It's always good just plain pickled.

. . .

Make this salad in early summer when baby beets, carrots, potatoes, and lettuces are just coming to market. If they're small and tender, you'll only have to scrub the carrots, beets, and potatoes—no peeling necessary. Just the potatoes and eggs require cooking; the carrots and beets will soften in the dressing. Use a full-fat sour cream with no additives for the dressing; it blends better with the other ingredients. Since this dish needs to marinate up to two days, boil and chill the eggs the day you plan to serve the salad.

SALAD

1 (8-ounce) jar pickled herring

½ cup thinly sliced carrots

½ cup thinly sliced celery hearts

½ cup baby red potatoes, skin on, steamed, cut into quarter-inch pieces

¼ cup firm cucumber, peeled and seeded, cut into quarter-inch pieces

1 tart green-skinned apple, peeled and cored, cut into quarter-inch pieces

½ cup beets cut into quarter-inch pieces

DRESSING

1½ cups full-fat sour cream

½ teaspoon creamy horseradish

1 teaspoon white sugar

1 tablespoon white vinegar

1 small bunch fresh dillweed, half finely minced, half reserved for garnish

GARNISH

2 hard-cooked eggs

several small heads of baby lettuce

1. Place herring in a sieve or colander and drain; it's okay if some of the brine remains. Cut into half-inch pieces and set aside. In a large glass or ceramic bowl, combine all the cut salad ingredients with the herring pieces, mixing well.

2. Combine sour cream, horseradish, and sugar in a bowl; add vinegar and stir until smooth. Stir in minced dillweed.

3. Pour the dressing over the salad ingredients and fold in with a rubber spatula. Cover bowl tightly with plastic wrap and refrigerate for up to 2 days; stir once or twice during that time so flavors blend. Wrap the remainder of the dill in paper towel, seal in a plastic bag, and refrigerate for use as a garnish when serving.

4. To serve: cut cooked eggs in half, remove yolks from whites, and mash yolks and chop whites separately; set aside. Gently rinse small lettuce heads, shake off excess water, and cut through the core into quarters, leaving the core in place. Mince reserved dillweed fronds; set aside. Uncover the herring salad and place in a large, shallow serving bowl or on a platter. Place lettuce quarters around the edge of the dish, with core ends tucked under the salad. Garnish the top of the salad with alternating stripes of mashed egg yolk and chopped egg whites; sprinkle minced dill over the whites.

SLICED RADISH SALAD

[serves 4]

In late summer, sliced garden salads appeared on nearly everyone's table. But the sliced salad eaten in one house might be totally different from the sliced salad the next-door neighbors were having. Everyone had a version, generally based on which roots and vines grew in their gardens, what point the growing season was at, and the variety of herbs and types of vinegars and oils familiar to them. The Italians sliced zucchini, fennel, peppers, and tomatoes and dressed them with homemade red wine vinegar and olive oil, fresh basil, and oregano. The Germans made their salads with sliced turnips and kohlrabi or cucumbers and dill or tarragon doused with cider vinegar and little, if any, oil. Swedes and Norwegians weighed in with beets and potatoes, radishes and cucumbers sluiced with caraway-laced white vinegar.

. . .

Eventually, as others' ingredients became familiar, some of the combinations began to comingle. This version is a loose marriage between the Swedes and the Germans, with a little Italian and French thrown in to liven things up. It's very light visually and would pair well with—or on—some lightly smoked fish and water crackers, accompanied by a light, dry white or sparkling wine.

Use a mandoline or a very sharp vegetable peeler or thin-bladed knife to get the thin vegetable slices that make this a light, pliable salad. There are no precise measurements for the vinegar or oil; just add a light spritzing of each.

3–4 large red radishes	1 bunch tarragon
2 small white turnips	champagne vinegar
1 small fennel bulb, with the fronds	light olive or canola oil
	flaked or fine-grained sea salt

1. Scrub and trim radishes, turnips, and fennel bulb. Remove stalks from fennel; reserve the fronds. Spread a piece of parchment or waxed paper over your working surface. Using a mandoline or a peeler or knife, slice all vegetables as thinly as possible onto the paper without compacting; they should be pliable and translucent; try keeping them in orderly piles.

2. Gently pull fennel fronds apart and strip leaves from tarragon; set aside in light piles.

3. Carefully transfer layers of each vegetable to 4 slightly chilled salad plates, arranging so vegetables overlap one another. Scatter the fennel fronds and tarragon leaves over the plates. Sprinkle each with vinegar, then oil, followed by a light dusting of salt, and serve.

PANZANELLA / BREAD SALAD

[serves 6–8]

In late summer, this was a go-to dish for using up small leftovers: dried bread ends, bits of meat and cheese, cooked beans. Because it needs to sit to develop the right flavor and consistency, it's also a great salad to make in the morning and take to work for a light, energizing lunch. Panzanella is a great way to use up some of those not-quite-ripe store-bought winter tomatoes, when you're tired of the canned ones and craving that juicy, vine-ripened texture and taste.

Consider this recipe to be a starting point. Delicious with these few basic components, your salad won't be ruined by adding one or two other items. Use ingredients that complement the flavor and add to the texture, like bits of cured meats, small cubes of cheese, whole cooked beans like favas or garbanzos; it's a good place for those dribs and drabs, with a nod to that parsimonious Range mantra: throw nothing away. Remove most of the liquid and seeds when cutting the tomatoes; enough juice will be generated while the salad rests. The bread should be dry, at least a day or two old. Don't trim the crusts; the salad should have a somewhat chewy texture. Be a bit sparing with the salt when first seasoning: you want the salad to have a nice, soft texture, not a mushy one. You can add more salt to taste before serving.

3–4 large vine-ripened tomatoes, cut in large pieces (4 cups)

4 cups day-old dry Italian or French bread, cut into 1-inch pieces

1 large cucumber, peeled and seeded, cut into 1-inch pieces

1 small red onion, cut into half-inch pieces

>>

1 bunch fresh basil, torn into small pieces	freshly ground pepper
¼–½ cup extra-virgin olive oil	**FOR SERVING**
sea or kosher salt	romaine hearts, torn, optional

1. Mix everything together in a large glass or ceramic bowl, cover, and let sit at room temperature in a moderately cool, dry place for 30 minutes or up to 12 hours. Do not refrigerate.

2. Serve in shallow bowls at room temperature, with torn romaine hearts if desired.

Cook's Notes: If you don't have two- or three-day old bread, cut fresh crusty bread—end pieces are best—into 1-inch cubes, evenly spread on an unrimmed baking sheet, and put in a preheated 300-degree oven for 5 to 10 minutes; the cut sides should be dry but not brown. Large green olives with pits, like Cerignola, and small, fresh mozzarella balls—bocconcini—are nice additions as well.

SOUPS

TESSY'S CHICKEN SOUP

[serves 8]

Tessy says, "I graduated from high school in Hibbing in 1943, but I started cooking when I was fourteen. The first thing I learned to cook, I think, was chicken soup. I learned to cook from my mother, and she learned to cook from her mother, who was a very good cook. My mother was also a very good cook. Everyone liked her cooking, but she was busy. During the Depression she worked in the drugstore with her father who started it; it was a Rexall store. My grandfather was a very kind man. People were poor, especially out in the country. Lots of them couldn't afford to pay for their medicine when they came into town, but my grandfather never refused anyone. He would have them sign the bill, and keep it so they could pay him when they had the money. After he died and my mother and her sisters were cleaning things up, they found all sorts of bills and records under the cash register that were marked with people's names and how they paid. Some paid in cash, some paid in fresh vegetables, and some paid in chickens; our family was never hungry.

"This is my mother's recipe; it's a classic. You need an old stewing hen. Some people think they're tough, but they have the most flavor. Wash the chicken and vegetables thoroughly; take off most of the fat and use it to make *schmaltz* [page 109]."

. . .

A clear broth is the hallmark of a good chicken soup; Tessy advises "use cold water that's been run for a while so it is clean and clear, and never let it boil." For best results, use a fine-mesh strainer that will sit securely over the top of a bowl large enough to contain the broth without touching the bottom of the bowl; line with three layers of damp cheesecloth. Using a ladle, slowly strain the broth to catch any residue that you missed in skimming; pouring broth directly from the pot will result in a cloudy appearance.

In a modern twist on her mother's classic, Tessy said sometimes she cuts some of the chicken in small pieces and puts it in the strained broth, then uses an immersion blender "to make it a nice, creamy soup because, you know, sometimes, once in a while, you want a little change."

1 (4–5 pound) stewing hen, older is better	2 carrots, scrubbed and cut in chunks, plus additional slices for garnish
12 cups cold water	
1 teaspoon kosher salt	4 celery ribs with tops, cut in chunks
1 large yellow onion, cut in chunks	minced parsley for garnish

1. Rinse the chicken thoroughly; trim off excess fat and set aside to render into *schmaltz* (see page 109); halve or quarter chicken. Put water in a stockpot and stir in salt to dissolve; add chicken, cover, place over high heat, and *just* bring to a boil—keep a close eye. Once it starts to boil, uncover immediately and lower the heat to a simmer. Never let it boil longer than a few seconds so the broth stays clear. >>

2. Add onions, carrots, and celery. Simmer, uncovered, until the chicken is tender, about 3 hours, skimming when necessary. The broth should be clear with a slight golden color when done.

3. Carefully lift chicken out of the stockpot, letting broth drain off, and place on a platter. Slowly ladle the broth through a fine-mesh strainer into a bowl, along with any from platter; cover with plastic wrap or a plate, leaving a small opening, and refrigerate. When cool, wrap and refrigerate the chicken and save for another use, such as chicken salad or a garnish for the broth.

4. To serve, remove broth from refrigerator and lift off any fat that may have solidified on the top. Heat until warm, and serve with matzoh balls or *Kreplach* (page 134); garnish with a few thin carrot slices or some minced parsley, if desired.

BEEF *MÔJAKKA*

[serves 6–8 generously]

This is a classic stew-like boiled dinner—pronounced *mo-ie-yak-ka*—using what was at hand at the moment. There are many versions found in the Scandinavian and Finnish-Baltic cultures, some with onions, others with rutabaga, and sometimes fish in place of meat—it just depended on where it was made, the time of year, and what was available.

Lila Suomu Johnson, age eighty-eight, recalled, "And then my mother taught me *môjakka.* Hers was potatoes and meat, beef mostly from our cows, but sometimes lamb if she could get some. She would put onion or little bit carrot in, too. And she'd give us some of the dried bread that she'd saved up to dunk in the juice; oh that was good."

* * *

To make *môjakka* you'll need a large enamel kettle or stainless steel stockpot, one deep enough for the water to boil straight up and not over the top while blanching the meat or fish and enough room left to hold all the vegetables you'll be adding later. This could be called the Baltic equivalent of Jewish chicken soup combined with French consommé: the end broth *is* the soup; everything else is just garnish.

12 cups cold water

1 pound beef stew meat (see notes), patted dry

8–10 skin-on baby red potatoes, halved or quartered

8–10 slender skin-on green-top carrots; tops removed, carrots scrubbed and cut into bite-size pieces

10–15 fresh or frozen pearl onions, peeled

4 small turnips, scrubbed, peeled, and cut into bite-size pieces

1 medium rutabaga, peeled and cut into bite-size pieces

4–5 tender inner celery stalks, including the hearts with their leaves, cut into bite-size pieces

a cheesecloth sachet bag containing

  1 tablespoon black peppercorns

  1–2 teaspoons whole allspice

  4–5 bay leaves

kosher or sea salt

handful flat-leaf Italian parsley, coarsely chopped, for garnish

1. Place the cold water into a large stockpot, add the beef, and bring to a rolling boil for 20 minutes; skim off foam and any meat particles that rise to the top until broth is clear. Turn off heat, remove meat, cut into bite-size pieces, and set aside. Cover the broth with a piece of cheesecloth or paper towel to pick up any remaining particles that have risen to the top; use another wet paper towel to remove any scum from around the inside edge.

2. Return the meat to the pot along with the prepared vegetables and the sachet bag. Bring to a boil, reduce heat, and simmer until meat and vegetables are tender, about 20 minutes. Taste for salt, adding more if desired. Remove from heat, carefully transfer to a smaller stainless steel or glass container, and cool for 20 minutes. Cover and refrigerate overnight with the sachet bag in place.*

3. To serve, remove the sachet bag, ladle soup into a saucepan, and reheat over medium. Garnish with Italian parsley.

Cook's Notes: *The equivalent amount of lamb or firm coldwater white fish, like Baltic cod or northern pike, may be substituted for the beef. The cooking time for fish is half that for meat but long enough to soften any bones—especially northern pike—overlooked in the fillets. Patting the beef dry helps seal in the juices, resulting in a clearer broth with less scum. Serve with Sliced Radish Salad (page 114) and hardtack (page 18) or Potato Rolls (page 29), with lots of sweet cream butter.*

*Môjakka is always better if it rests overnight in the refrigerator, but you can eat it right off the stove if you can't wait.

THURSDAY PEA SOUP
WITH GINGER, ORANGE, AND SMOKED HAM

[serves 6–8]

This pea soup is more than *just* the thick soup that sustained Scandinavians through endless dark winters. On a late winter day many years ago, the hearty peasant fare became an accidental, elegant feast in my great-aunt's kitchen. She decided her soup was too thin, and last fall's potatoes were getting low—as was the flour bin—so how was she to thicken it? In the old country, her mother would break stale bread into pieces to thicken soup and gravy, but my great-aunt wanted to save the bread in the cupboard until she could bake more. Then she remembered: after Christmas she had hidden some ginger cookies away from her two sons in case unexpected company came by; she would use those. The crumbled cookies elevated an everyday supper into an unexpected banquet. Her husband and sons ate every last bit and asked her to make more. Ginger in pea soup became a family standard.

. . .

I use grated fresh gingerroot in my pea soup, something not available to my grandmother and great-aunts, and add the juice and zest of a fresh orange, which brightens the flavor. A good smoked pork hock or piece of dry-cured ham pairs well with the spice and sweet. Using whole dried peas gives the soup a better texture; they'll need to soak in water overnight. These can be found in co-ops, Scandinavian specialty shops, and some grocery stores, but the soup can be made with split peas; no soaking is necessary. Tradition has Thursday as the day to eat a supper of pea soup with a ham bone in it, followed by Swedish Pancakes (page 51) with Lingonberry Sauce (page 53), but I think you'll be just as happy with the suggestions at the end of the recipe.

1 pound whole dried peas (see head note)

6–8 cups low-sodium chicken or beef stock, or a combination of the two

1 large (2-pound) smoked pork hock

a cheesecloth sachet*
containing:

   3–4 whole cloves

   1 large yellow onion, peeled
   and quartered

   2-inch piece fresh gingerroot,
   peeled and halved lengthwise

   1 large carrot, peeled and
   halved lengthwise

   1 rib celery, halved
   lengthwise

   3–4 parsley stems, tops
   reserved for garnish

1 bay leaf

1 large navel orange or 2
clementines, zest reserved
for garnish, fruit quartered

2 teaspoons dried thyme leaves
or 1 tablespoon fresh

kosher or sea salt and freshly
ground pepper

for garnish:

   2 thin carrots, peeled and cut
   into thin coins

   reserved parsley tops,
   minced

   reserved orange zest

*For the aromatic bundle, use enough string to tie a looped end to the pot handle while the bundle is submerged, making removal easy.

1. Pour peas into a shallow bowl or rimmed baking sheet; sort through and remove any withered peas or stones. Place in a strainer or colander and rinse under cold running water. Put in a deep bowl or pot—peas should only fill one-quarter of the container. Add cold water to fill container halfway; cover and refrigerate overnight.

2. In the morning, drain and rinse the peas and place in a large stockpot or slow cooker. Add the stock and pork hock. Insert cloves into onion quarters; wrap with other aromatics (gingerroot through orange) in cheesecloth and tie with string. Firmly squeeze bundle over the pot to release fruit and vegetable juices, and bury in the peas. Add thyme, 2 teaspoons salt, and several grinds of pepper. Bring to a boil, reduce heat, and simmer for 1½ to 2 hours (4 to 5 in a slow cooker).

3. While the soup is cooking, place sliced carrots, minced parsley, and orange zest in a small bowl. Add boiling water just to cover, and let steep for 5 minutes. Strain water into the soup, then rinse carrots, parsley, and zest under cold water to fix the color; set aside.

4. When the peas are tender, remove aromatic bundle and discard. Remove pork hock to a cutting board and let cool; then remove meat from bones and finely chop. Remove about one-third of the soup to a blender or food processor; blend until smooth and return to the pot with the chopped pork. Taste for seasoning and adjust as needed. Serve in bowls topped with reserved garnish.

>>

Cook's Notes: With the addition of a rye bread like Swedish Limpa (page 20) or Söt Sur Bröd (page 22), Havarti cheese and dill pickles, Radish Salad (page 114), and rice pudding (page 168) with Spicy Swedish Ginger Thins (page 157), you'll have a Scandinavian winter feast that will satisfy every family and all company.

Wild Natural Resources

The northern Minnesota lakes and forests were lifesavers for immigrants, providing abundant fish and game to sustain families in the early days after they arrived. Setting up gardens would take time, as would adapting to an abbreviated growing season in a climate that couldn't support the warm-weather, plant-based diets to which many immigrants were accustomed. Wild protein alone wasn't going to suffice. Drawing on knowledge and instinct, savvy Italians and Slavs took to the fields and forests, just as they'd done for generations in the balmy homelands they'd left behind, and found a cold-weather cornucopia to bridge this dietary gap.

From the last frost in spring to the first frost in the fall, they gathered what they knew were safe mushrooms, herbs, berries, fruits, and vegetables. Well into the 1960s, elderly immigrants could be seen combing the woods and patrolling railroad beds for wild mushrooms, asparagus, and sorrel. Dandelion greens were an easy target starting in the spring and continuing into summer. June brought strawberries, followed by blueberries, blackberries, raspberries, and currants through the end of July.

Wild plums, apples, and grapes; rosehips and some late mushrooms and horseradish; hazelnuts, currants, and highbush cranberries rounded out the season, filling pantries and root cellars with canned and dried fruit, jams and jellies, and even dandelion, wild grape, and chokecherry wines to warm families in the cold winter nights they were certain lay ahead.

• • •

I'd be remiss if I didn't acknowledge the two important wild natural resources the northern regions have to offer: wild rice and maple syrup.

Minnesota leads the nation in true wild rice production and comes second or third in the country in the manufacturing of maple syrup. The Minnesota Department of Natural Resources has regulation guidelines for private residents and nonresidents; permits and licenses are required and apply to specific areas of the state. All native wild rice within the existing boundaries of the Minnesota Indian reservations is managed by the respective reservation wild rice committees.

Information, current schedules, and regulations on wild rice and maple syrup harvesting are available at www.dnr.state.mn.us/index.html.

Men eating pasta in Valentini's Supper Club, Chisholm, Minnesota. Left to right: Albie Stanager, Ken Rudstrom, Gene Cawley

SIDES

DOUBLE BOILER POLENTA

[serves 10–12]

In addition to stretching small amounts of meat to feed large hungry families in times of financial hardship, the ever-resourceful Italian wives and mothers kept hunger at bay by cooking big batches of polenta. It required a good amount of stirring to be fully cooked, but two cups of dry cornmeal would mushroom into enough polenta to feed a family of eight to ten; doubled or tripled, it could take them through several days. The first serving from a fresh batch was eaten straight from the pot, soft and creamy, skillfully flavored with bits of leftover meats, cheeses, or vegetables. The rest would be spread on an oiled pan, chilled until firm, then cut into pieces, wrapped in oiled paper, and refrigerated—ready at a moment's notice when hungry children and husbands wandered in from the garden or yard. Fried in a little olive oil to get a nice crust, then topped with the last of the gravy or tomato sauce from yesterday or the day before, it was almost like having Sunday dinner two days in a row.

. . .

Good polenta—like risotto—takes time. The traditional method could be compared to a rhythmic meditation: cooking slowly, constantly stirring, softening the grains and bringing out their deep flavors and creamy textures. Today time is short, and sometimes following tradition isn't an option, but the Italians came up with a method to manage that sort of deprivation, too. It still takes a while, but making polenta in a double boiler has removed most of the standing and stirring—with an equally satisfying outcome. You'll need a large (6–8 quart) stainless steel bowl, a 1-quart pot, and a 6-quart pot large enough to securely set the bowl over without touching the water below or slipping off, a sturdy, balloon-type stainless steel whisk, and a large stainless steel spoon.

3 cups water, stock, or a combination of water and milk	1 cup cornmeal
salt	bits of cooked meat, grated cheese, minced herbs, or diced, cooked vegetables, optional

1. Pour the cooking liquid into a 1-quart pot, bring to a boil, and add a generous pinch of salt. Fill a 6-quart pot one-third with water and heat to a simmer. Place a large stainless steel bowl on a piece of rubber matting or a damp, folded dish towel large enough to hold it in place while stirring the cornmeal. Transfer the boiling liquid to the bowl and *slowly* pour the cornmeal in with one hand while *vigorously* whisking with the other to prevent lumps from forming.

2. Tightly cover bowl with aluminum foil and set over the simmering water to cook for at least 1½ hours, stirring several times with the whisk during the first 20 minutes and only once or twice every 20 minutes after. Keep an eye on the simmering water, adding more as necessary. Taste each time you stir to check for salt, bitterness, and texture. Add more salt if needed, and continue to cook until the bitterness is gone and the polenta is tender, up to 30 minutes longer.

3. Add any flavoring ingredients, and serve in shallow dishes; the polenta will stay soft for several hours if covered and held over hot water. Spread remaining, still-warm polenta on a rimmed baking sheet brushed with olive oil; cool to room temperature, cover, and refrigerate. When chilled it can be sliced, wrapped, and refrigerated for up to 5 days. Reheat by sautéing, grilling, or baking.

Cook's Notes: *This is a great side with* Braciole *(page 83) and spinach or Swiss chard sautéed with lots of garlic. Top with spicy red sauce (page 130) or sautéed mushrooms and onions, or raid your refrigerator—the possibilities are endless.*

Polenta alla Spianatora / The Polenta Board

One of the more endearing family food traditions Italians brought to the Iron Range was *Polenta alla Spianatora,* the polenta board. In Italy, meat had always been a precious luxury for large families, reserved for celebrations and special occasions, and things were no different for Italian immigrants in the early days on the Range. Justina Valentini brought this tradition to Chisholm and her restaurant, Valentini's Supper Club, instilling it in her family, who keep it alive today.

Each year on the day after Thanksgiving, Nello Valentini and Orlando Bonicelli would stir up a large batch of polenta in Justina's restaurant kitchen and spread it on the surface of a smooth, clean door that had been secured over the top of a large table in the back dining room. Homemade *sugo* would be spread over the surface and small bits of savory meats, usually a combination of pork and beef, some sausages and some roasts, were placed in the center of the polenta. Everyone would position themselves around the board, where each was given a spoon. The children occupied the more advantageous positions along the long side edges of the door to compensate for their shorter arms, while the adults stationed themselves on the ends. When the scorekeeper announced the start, everyone began eating at the same time, racing to be the first to eat their way into the center of the polenta and claim the bits of meat as their prize.

The Valentinis continued this tradition in the restaurant until it was sold to an outside party in the early part of this century. The second generation keeps *Polenta alla Spianatora* alive at family gatherings.

DANISH SUGAR-BROWNED POTATOES

[serves 6]

Sugar with potatoes? The combination may seem oxymoronic, but in this dish the two go together like a potato hand in a sugar glove. Elegant in appearance with a sweet amber lacquer, these potatoes are always present at Danish celebration meals and are the perfect side to Crackling Roast Pork (page 92) with its salty, crisp exterior.

. . .

Use small, thin-skinned yellow flesh potatoes—Yukon Gold, Klondike, or Yellow Finn—the newer the better. Once boiled and cooled, the skins slip off easily, and the creamy, firm texture stays intact when they're rolled and shaken in the sugar and butter mixture.

1½ pounds small, firm yellow flesh potatoes [see head note]	3 tablespoons unsalted butter
salt	freshly cracked pepper and coarse sea salt, optional
3 tablespoons white sugar	

1. Carefully scrub the potatoes, taking care not to remove any skin. Place in a deep empty pot, cover with cold water, and bring to a boil. Once water is boiling add a generous pinch of salt and cook potatoes until just tender (test with the tip of a sharp knife or the prongs of a fork), about 15 to 20 minutes. Remove from the heat, carefully drain in a colander, and rinse under cold, running water until cool enough to pick up by hand. Peel off the skins, rinse potatoes in cold water, and set aside in colander to drain.

2. Place a heavy skillet over medium heat, add sugar, and stir with a heatproof rubber spatula until sugar has dissolved and is light brown at the edges. Add the butter and stir until it is melted and incorporated into the sugar.

3. Shake the colander to remove excess water from the potatoes, and carefully slide them into the pan (adding them too quickly can cause the hot butter-sugar mixture to spatter). Carefully roll the potatoes in the mixture until completely coated. Continue to shake the pan and roll the potatoes until they are warmed through and evenly glazed with a light to medium amber color, about 10 minutes.

4. If desired, sprinkle with a bit of freshly cracked pepper and coarse, large-grained sea salt while the coating on the potatoes is still liquid.

POTATO RUTABAGA SOUFFLÉ

[serves 6–8]

Rutabagas are one of the most maligned vegetables grown, and it's a bad rap. Try rutabagas in this combination. Just call it by its *nom de plume*—soufflé—and you'll get this one past your doubting family and guests, no questions asked, and be showered with praise. Rutabagas are sometimes sold with a wax coating, as a way to keep them from becoming soft over several months of storage. Though they'll last when held in a cool, dark, dry environment, it's best to buy them unwaxed in late fall or early winter. Choose small, firm rutabagas; younger and thinner skinned, they are sweeter and have a smoother mouthfeel than the larger ones, which can sometimes be on the bitter side with a wooden texture.

1 cup finely chopped red onion	1 cup half-and-half
4 tablespoons [½ stick] unsalted butter, melted, divided	1 cup freshly grated Parmesan cheese, divided
1 cup unseasoned bread crumbs, divided	6 tablespoons finely chopped parsley, divided
3 cups cooked, mashed baking potatoes	2 teaspoons salt
3 cups cooked, mashed rutabaga	1½ teaspoons white pepper
4 large eggs	½ teaspoon freshly grated nutmeg, optional

>>

1. Preheat oven to 375 degrees; place rack in center. Cook the minced onion in 1 tablespoon of melted butter, stirring frequently. Let cool.

2. Grease an 8-cup soufflé or casserole dish with ½ tablespoon of the melted butter, and cover buttered surface with one-third of the bread crumbs. Set aside.

3. Place mashed potatoes and rutabaga in a large mixing bowl, and mix until thoroughly combined. In a separate bowl, beat eggs together with half-and-half, ¼ cup Parmesan cheese, and 2 tablespoons minced parsley. Add the onions, salt, pepper, and nutmeg (if using), mix well, and add mixture to potatoes and rutabaga. Beat with a wooden spoon for 1 to 2 minutes; this step will help the potato mixture rise a bit in the oven.

4. Turn mixture into prepared casserole or soufflé dish. Place remaining melted butter, bread crumbs, Parmesan cheese, and minced parsley in the mixing bowl, stir to combine, and spread on top of the soufflé. Bake for 30 to 40 minutes. The mixture should puff up a bit and be golden brown on top.

MA SPADACCINI'S ITALIAN BEANS IN TOMATO SAUCE

[serves 6]

Rosy Cummings's parents arrived on the Iron Range from the Abruzzi region of Italy. Her father—Sam "Pa" Spadaccini—was a natural gardener who would become one of Hibbing's unofficial horticulturalists, and her mother—Maria Nicole "Ma" Spadaccini—a cook whose abilities were unparalleled. The volumes of fruits and vegetables Pa was able to coax from a small space that was more miniature truck farm than everyday backyard garden are hard to comprehend. With ground space at a premium, the only way to grow was up. Thick grapevines wove through a wire fence that ran the length of the yard; Italian pole beans towered over tomatoes, green and banana peppers, and leafy Swiss chard; and zucchini vines wound around garlic scapes and onion tops. Inside a kitchen so small that two people were in each other's way, Rosy and her sister Mary helped their mother transform their father's bounty into family meals of the moment and the full larder that would feed them well into winter. Ma Spadaccini was a good teacher, and her lessons in the classics continue on with her grandchildren and great-grandchildren.

· · ·

Late summer: a garden overflowing with more sun-ripened beans and tomatoes, cauliflower and broccoli than the family of six could possibly consume straight from stem and vine meant it was time to make antipasto (page 98). Amid high-priority canning projects, regular meals had to be made too, but they had to be fast. Except for the olive oil, salt, and pepper, everything in this classic dish came directly out of Rosy's father's garden. Flat Italian green pole beans can be found at farmers markets and in some grocery stores in late summer. If you can't find fresh beans, Rosy recommends using canned, not frozen, to get the right texture. Simple to make—the way her mother taught her—she says these are "Hmmm, Hmmm Good!"

1 tablespoon good olive oil	salt and pepper
½ green pepper, cut into quarter-inch pieces	2 cans (about 2 pounds) Italian pole beans (see head note)
3 large cloves garlic, minced	Romano cheese
1 cup tomato sauce or 1 (8-ounce) can Roma tomatoes	

Heat oil in a large skillet until shimmering. Add green pepper and garlic and cook, stirring; don't let garlic brown. Add the tomato sauce and salt and pepper to taste; cover and simmer for 30 minutes. Add the beans and cook, covered, until tender; about 15 minutes for canned and 40 minutes for fresh. Serve with freshly grated Romano cheese.

Cook's Notes: *These are delicious at room temperature with crusty Italian bread and a good green olive oil. Some homemade Italian red wine like Rosy's father made from his grapes goes great with these, too!*

IL SUGO CON POMODORI ARROSTITI / OVEN-ROASTED TOMATO SAUCE

[makes enough to feed a crowd]

I'd like to tell you that this recipe was for someone's treasured family red sauce that had been guardedly passed from generation to generation, starting a century or two ago back in Naples or Sicily, where there had been a great-great-grandmother who had verbally transferred ownership of it to her daughter, who entrusted it to her daughter as she made her way to America with it, the Midwest to be specific, and one of the many Italian communities on the Iron Range to be even more specific, where it was finally written down and eventually ended up in the recipe box of the great-great-granddaughter of the woman who started the whole chain of succession. *Capisce?*

But, no. It's the result of two twentieth-century, multiculti boomers—both Iron Range born and both good cooks: a half second-generation Swede-Finn/half third-generation English-Scotch-Irish-Franco-Germanic blend and another half second-generation Swede-Finn/half second-generation Abruzzese—okay so they've got a little Italian cred there. This recipe, if you will, was an accident of convenience, or maybe opportunity, sprouting in contemporary times with a few roots on the boot. And the Swede-Finn-Italian did spend a lot of time in the kitchen with his *nonna*, who spoke very little English but was a very good cook, and an even better teacher.

Try it in late summer, when you're overloaded with ripe tomatoes of any and all varieties. It's fast and it's easy; no water baths or pressure cookers involved. All you'll need for special equipment are several large rimmed baking sheets or broiler pans, a good food mill that sits securely over a large bowl, a second large bowl or kettle, and a few sheets of cooking parchment.

Roast the tomatoes in batches, two pans in the oven at a time, and don't crowd the roasting pans: leave some space between the tomatoes; you want the skins to blister and maybe brown a little. With preparation and organization, one person should be able to handle this method without too much difficulty, but two as a tag team will make everything go a lot faster. Because the water and flesh content vary in tomatoes, it's difficult to estimate in portions how much *sugo* you will have when all is said and done. You'll have enough for several polenta parties (see page 125), and then some.

10 pounds ripe tomatoes, any variety, rinsed, larger cores and bruised spots removed

1–2 large heads garlic, excess loose skin removed

2–3 bunches *Genovese* basil leaves and thin stems, woody stalks and roots trimmed

1 large bunch Italian parsley leaves and thin stems

1 cup good extra-virgin olive oil, plus more for parchment

coarse sea salt

red pepper flakes

OPTIONAL ADDITIONS

1 bunch lemon thyme, pulled into several small branches, leaves bruised, roots snapped off

1 bunch fresh rosemary, branches broken in pieces, needles bruised

1–2 bunches Italian (not Mexican) oregano, leaves and stems, broken in pieces

1–2 bay leaves, broken

1. Preheat oven to 450 or 500 degrees. Use the tip of a sharp knife to slash an X on the bottoms of the tomatoes; this will help the skins blister while roasting. Place in a large bowl or kettle, or a washtub if you have one and want to season all the tomatoes at the same time.

2. Smash garlic bulbs so cloves come off and skins rupture a little. Add to tomatoes along with the herbs, including any optional additions, olive oil, and salt and pepper to taste. If mixed in batches, portion the seasoning ingredients as evenly as possible; it doesn't need to be exact because the sauce from all the pans will be combined at the end. Mix together so ingredients are well distributed and coated with oil. Spread in batches over rimmed baking sheets or broiler pans in single layers, leaving some space among ingredients (see head note). Lightly oil lengths of parchment that will cover pans; loosely lay over tomatoes, oiled side–down.

3. Place 2 pans in oven at a time, one at the lowest level, the other two-thirds up; leave plenty of space between racks. Roast for 10 minutes, stir ingredients and redistribute, switch rack positions, and roast for an additional 10 minutes or until tomatoes start to blister.

>>

4. While the first batch is roasting, set a large bowl in the sink and attach the food mill. When the first batch comes out of the oven, scoop into second bowl or kettle. Refill pans with additional tomatoes and herbs; cover with same parchment, unless it is brittle and breaks into pieces, then replace with another. Place pans in oven to roast, as you did for the first.

5. While the second batch is roasting, scoop warm tomato mixture into the food mill and press into the bowl. When the first "load" has been pressed through, scrape sauce from the bottom side of the mill into the bowl, then scrape skins, stems, and seeds from the inside into a trash or other container. Refill the food mill, and repeat until all tomatoes have been pushed through. By this point, the next batch should be ready to come out of the oven.

6. Once all tomatoes have been roasted and processed, combine all batches of sauce, stir well, taste for seasoning, and adjust as needed. Line up freezer containers close together on a counter or tabletop; use a large-mouthed canning funnel if you have one, and ladle or pour sauce from a large measuring cup into the containers, leaving a quarter inch or more for headroom: sauce will expand a bit as it freezes. Freeze in single layers if you have room, and stack when frozen solid.

Cook's Notes: *Congratulations: you now have a basic sauce base to cover all manner of meals, from soups, polentas, pastas (Carmela's Ravioli, page 75), meats (Braciole, page 83), pizzas, and hot sandwiches to whatever else your appetite might desire. Use at this thickness for soup; reduce for sauces. Adjust and modify seasonings for individual dishes and your personal tastes. Buon appetito!*

KNISHES

[makes about 24 knishes]

This recipe was shared with me by Tessy Oxman. It came from her husband David's Ukrainian-born great-grandmother, who brought it with her when she came to Duluth from Russia in the late 1880s. Tessy told me it was a very old-world recipe, and the method for making the knishes is, too. The technique is specific but not hard. You want the dough as thin as possible but still sturdy enough to keep the filling in; a good, tight seal helps with that, too. Cold mashed potatoes are called for here, so plan ahead: it's a good place to use leftovers. Tessy serves these with ketchup.

DOUGH

2 cups all-purpose flour

1 teaspoon baking powder

½ cup vegetable shortening

1 large egg, beaten

½ teaspoon kosher salt

½ cup boiling water

canola oil

FILLING

1 large onion, finely chopped

2 teaspoons to 1½ tablespoons canola oil

8 ounces lean ground beef, optional

2 cups mashed potatoes, chilled

⅓ teaspoon garlic powder

salt and pepper

flour

1 large egg, slightly beaten

1. For dough, mix together flour, baking powder, shortening, egg, and salt. Add water, combine thoroughly, and form mixture into a ball; rub with a few drops of canola oil. Cover in plastic wrap and refrigerate for 1 hour.

2. For the filling, cook onion in a little oil until lightly browned. If including ground beef, add to cooked onions with remaining oil and brown; drain excess oil into a small dish and set aside. Mix cooled potatoes with onion and beef (if using), garlic powder, and salt and pepper to taste. Set aside.

3. Preheat oven to 375 degrees. Sprinkle cutting board or countertop with a little flour. Remove dough from refrigerator and divide into 3 pieces. Place one piece

>>

of dough on the floured surface and roll into a very thin rectangle, about 5 x 14 inches.

4. Place a 1-inch-thick row of potato mixture down the length of the dough, leaving a ½- to ¾-inch outer edge uncovered. Fold edge over filling and tightly roll up lengthwise, as for a jelly roll; pinch edge lengthwise to seal.

5. Flour the side of your hand and cut the dough into 1½- to 2-inch pieces by pressing into the roll, quickly moving back and forth in a sawing motion. Tightly pinch ends together to seal.

6. Place each knish on one end and flatten down slightly with your fingertips. Set knishes on a greased baking sheet and brush tops with beaten egg and reserved oil. Bake for about 25 minutes or until brown on the bottom and top. Serve hot.

Cook's Notes: *Knishes are delicious plain; or serve with ketchup, a little spicy brown mustard, or creamy horseradish on the side.*

קרעפּלעך / *KREPLACH*

[makes 36 dumplings]

Similar to Italian ravioli or Chinese wontons, *kreplach* are small, triangle-shaped, traditional Yiddish dumplings filled with ground beef and onion or mashed potatoes and served in chicken soup. They're usually boiled before being added to the broth but can be deep-fried and served as a side to chicken soup or on their own. Today's cooks may use frozen wonton wrappers, which are better fried than boiled, but not as traditional.

• • •

This recipe for *kreplach* is adapted from one by Ann Sher, which was included in the 1981 edition of *Hot off the Range,* compiled by the Jewish Women of the Hibbing-Chisholm Hadassah.

FILLING

1 pound ground beef

1 large egg, beaten

1 tablespoon grated yellow
onion

salt and pepper

½ cup water

DOUGH

4 large eggs

2 tablespoons cold water

2⅔ cups all-purpose flour

1. In a medium bowl, combine beef, egg, onion, and a sprinkle or more of salt and pepper. Stir in water, mix well, and refrigerate.

2. For the dough, in a medium bowl, beat eggs and water together. Add flour until dough is of rolling consistency, not sticky; divide into 4 equal pieces. On a lightly floured surface, roll out one piece of dough into a very thin square— about ⅛ inch thick; cut into 2-inch squares. Carefully separate the squares so there is an inch between each.

3. Put about ¼ teaspoon of the chilled meat mixture on each square, toward one corner. Brush edges of dough with a little water. Fold dough over meat to form a triangle; seal by pressing moistened edges together. Repeat with remaining dough pieces and filling.

4. Place dumplings in a large pot of boiling, salted water; leave enough room so dumplings cook without sticking to each other; and cook for about 20 minutes; drain well. Add three or four to chicken soup (page 116), or serve as a side dish.

Cook's Notes: Make ahead in large batches, boil for about 5 minutes, and drain well, blotting with paper towels to remove excess moisture. Place in single layers on parchment-lined baking sheets and freeze; when solid, remove to zip-top bags and put in freezer. To serve, cook dumplings in boiling, salted water for several minutes before adding to soup broth.

CHAPTER 6

Desserts & Sweets

*Some people used to come here thinking
I was making strudel for a wedding,
but it was only for my family.*

MARY PERPICH
*MOTHER OF GOVERNOR RUDY PERPICH, AGE SEVENTY-FIVE,
HIBBING, MINNESOTA, FEBRUARY 1987*

Having something sweet available has always been an integral part of people's daily eating patterns, especially so with immigrants whose homey ends to everyday meals and traditional, often elaborate, conclusions to holiday, family, and religious celebrations went far beyond satisfying cravings. Almost more than the breads and savory dishes of their homelands, familiar pies, pastries, and confections served as touchstones and reminders of where people had come from, giving them comfort and identity in their new surroundings.

Sharing food, especially something sweet, was a natural course for the newcomers. Sweets could break down barriers; everyone liked them, and few would refuse a taste. These ethnic and traditional items reached out across the Iron Range, from social clubs and miner's lunch pails to church celebrations and holiday bazaars. They appeared as small bites at morning and afternoon coffee klatches with neighbors, at weekly card games and sewing circles, and at late-evening lunches with company.

Things haven't changed in the past century. It's always good to have something sweet on hand, no matter how meager, for after work, for after school, or to offer unexpected drop-ins. Everyone likes dessert.

MORMOR'S RHUBARB SAUCE

[serves 8–10]

My mother's first cousin, Linnea Eliason, was one of the earliest influences on my interest in food. While her sight is diminishing, her thoughts and sense of humor are firmly in place, if not more astute, and at age ninety-five she remains engaged and interested as ever in the world and people around her. She continues to be my mentor.

Linnea says, "When we lived in town my mother had a rhubarb bush and some onions. She always used that rhubarb and made sauce when it first came starting in June, but only until the end of July when it went to seed. There wasn't much room for her to have a garden, but once we were on the farm, *oh boy!*

"Every morning we had fresh farm eggs from the chickens, and milk from the cows when we got there in spring 1929, and coffee. It was so good. *Smokka! Var so gud!* My father and brothers had gone on ahead and put up the barn and the chicken coop, so things were ready for us when we got there. And we were lucky to be on the farm that fall in 1929 after Black Friday came. We were never hungry; we had good food, and we grew it all ourselves. And they planted *Mormor's** rhubarb bush that they took from town so she could make her sauce for us.

"And now that we had cows it was even better. We had one Guernsey cow that my father had gotten for us. Oh that Guernsey cow! She gave the best milk; better than all the other cows, especially in spring when she was eating the young grass and clover out in our pasture."

Linnea began to list all the things they made from the Guernsey's milk.

"We had whipped cream; in summer the cream was so thick the spoon would stand straight up in it *before* it was even whipped! Milk to make cheese and butter. Ice cream. Everything. We named her *Lil Un*† because she was the youngest, and she was so good. In spring, Mormor would make her rhubarb sauce, take it off the stove and put it in bowls with some of Lil Un's heavy cream

*Swedish: Mother's mother, or one's maternal grandmother. A term of respect often used as the familiar when one's own mother had become a grandmother.

†Swedish: Affectionate, colloquial name for small children.

over while it was still warm, and we would all go outside with our bowls and sit under the big Dolgo crabapple tree that would be blooming in our backyard, and eat it all up!"

. . .

The first rhubarb that comes up in the cool spring weather is the best; the thin, tender stalks are the most sour and juiciest. By midsummer the stalks toughen and dry up in the heat, and the plant goes to seed. Though it's really a vegetable, rhubarb is great for pies, muffins, crisps, and—of course—sauce, which is wonderful over ice cream, pancakes, and waffles or warmed and eaten alone under a soft blanket of heavy cream, dusted with brown sugar.

2 tablespoons salted butter	1 cup white sugar
6 cups thinly sliced rhubarb	pinch ginger or nutmeg

1. Melt butter in a large, heavy-bottomed saucepan over medium heat. Add rhubarb pieces; stir to coat with butter. Lower heat and cover with a tight-fitting lid. Cook for several minutes, until the rhubarb becomes very soft and starts to break down (see notes).

2. While rhubarb is cooking, mix sugar and ginger or nutmeg. Remove lid and stir sugar-spice mixture into the cooked rhubarb. Stirring constantly, cook until sugar dissolves and sauce begins to simmer and thicken; keep heat low, and continue to stir, scraping the bottom of the pan to keep the sauce from scorching, until it reaches desired consistency.

Cook's Notes: *Use a flame tamer to keep mixture from scorching (see head note page 106). Make this in large quantities in early spring when rhubarb is in peak season and freeze. Serve it over warm tapioca or rice pudding (page 168) with Spicy Swedish Ginger Thins (page 157) on the side.*

FRUIT SOUP

[serves 4–6]

Fruit soup was a way of incorporating small amounts of badly needed vitamin C into the winter diets of Scandinavians and Northern Europeans. The concentrated sweetness complemented by rich cream was a welcome departure from salty fish and dense breads. In most countries it was featured at holiday meals as breakfast and as a dessert.

1 cup chopped pitted prunes

1 cup chopped dried apricots

2 medium green apples, peeled and chopped

1 cinnamon stick

2 whole cloves

1½ cups water

1 tablespoon instant tapioca

2 tablespoons dry sherry

whipped or sour cream for garnish

1. In a 2-quart saucepan, combine prunes, apricots, apples, cinnamon stick, cloves, and water. Simmer for 20 minutes, or until the fruit is tender and the liquid is the consistency of thin syrup.

2. Stir in the instant tapioca and bring to a boil. Reduce heat to low and cook until the soup is slightly thickened, stirring with a wooden spoon to keep the fruit sugars from sticking to the bottom and burning.

3. Remove cinnamon stick and cloves. Stir in sherry. Serve in individual bowls with whipped or sour cream.

Perpich family at Carson Lake, outside Hibbing, Minnesota. Back: Mary and Anton. Front, left to right: Joe, George, Tony, and Rudy

MARY PERPICH'S APPLE STRUDEL

[serves 10–12]

Early twentieth-century immigrants brought strong work ethics, fueled by a determination not only to make a better life for themselves in their adopted homeland but to ensure their children would become full American citizens in their own rights. One of the better illustrations of this Iron Range resolve is Croatian immigrant Anton Prpić and his wife, Mary. With Croatian spoken exclusively at home, English became the second language for the eldest of their four sons when he started school. He and his next two brothers all became dentists, and in the 1970s all three served simultaneous terms as state representatives for neighboring Iron Range districts. The fourth brother followed a similar path, becoming a psychiatrist with an office practice in Washington, DC, at the same time the eldest was in office as the first Iron Range—and longest-serving—governor in Minnesota history. Was it just the gentle, firm pull of good parenting, or did a daily diet of their mother's handmade apple strudel figure into the mix?

• • •

This recipe appeared in the *New York Times* on February 25, 1987, when the oldest son, Rudy, was serving his second elected term as Minnesota's governor. "I made strudel every night," seventy-five-year-old Mary Perpich told an interviewer seated at her kitchen table in Hibbing. "By the end of the week I had peeled a bushel of apples. Some people used to come here thinking I was making strudel for a wedding, but it was only for my family."

Mary's recipe doesn't call for a specific pie apple, so I've adapted it to include three University of Minnesota–bred varieties that, like her sons, have grown to national prominence. Making the pastry takes a bit of skill, and beginners may want to ask friends to help stretch the dough, but with determination and practice even the novice can master Mary's technique; just be sure to take your rings off. When baking, use a conventional oven setting rather than a convection mode; the latter causes the pastry to brown before the apples are completely cooked.

3½ cups bread flour or unbleached all-purpose flour, divided, plus more for rolling

1 teaspoon salt

½ cup warmed vegetable oil, plus 2 tablespoons for bowl

2 large eggs, slightly beaten

⅔ cup warm water (105–115 degrees)

12 apples (Cortland, McIntosh, or Haralson or a combination), peeled, cored, and finely chopped

1–2 cups white sugar, depending on apples' tartness

2 teaspoons cinnamon

1 cup fresh bread crumbs

16 tablespoons (2 sticks) unsalted butter, melted

whipped cream or crème fraîche, for serving

1. Preheat oven or warming drawer to its lowest setting or 150 degrees. In a large bowl, combine 3 cups flour and salt, and make a well in the center. Add ½ cup oil, the beaten eggs, and warm water into the well; knead with your hands about 20 minutes, adding more flour if needed to make a soft but not sticky dough. Put remaining 2 tablespoons oil in a mixing bowl and add kneaded dough, turning to coat. Cover with plastic wrap or a dish towel, and place in the heated oven or warming drawer until the dough is warm and easy to pull, about 20 minutes.

2. On a table or other flat surface that is at least 3 x 5 feet, spread a clean bedsheet or large tablecloth so that the edges hang slightly over the sides. Lightly sprinkle the sheet with 1 to 2 tablespoons flour, and roll out the dough to form a 9 x 13–inch rectangle. Using your hands, start stretching and lifting the dough

>>

with your fingertips, pulling it out until you can see through it. When you are finished, the dough should cover the table's surface. Try to minimize the number of holes; a few won't matter.

3. Set oven at 350 degrees. While oven is heating, scatter the apples over the dough. Sprinkle with sugar, cinnamon, and bread crumbs. Drizzle about three-fourths of the melted butter over the mixture. Taking hold of the longer edge of the sheet, pull it up and over the apples, and continue to roll the dough around the filling jelly roll style. Using both hands, carefully lift the strudel and place seam side-down on a parchment-lined or greased jelly roll or low-sided baking pan; you may need to form the pastry into a large crescent to fit.* Brush the top of the strudel with remaining melted butter and bake for 50 to 60 minutes or until golden. If the strudel begins to brown too quickly, cover with aluminum foil. Serve warm with unsweetened whipped cream or room temperature crème fraîche.

*Strudel can be frozen at this point for up to three months. Do not butter the top. Wrap tightly in plastic. To bake: remove strudel from freezer, unwrap, and place, still frozen, on a rimmed baking sheet. Bake at 300 degrees for 30 minutes. Increase heat to 350 degrees, brush top with melted butter, and continue baking for 30 to 40 minutes.

MY MOTHER'S LUNCH BOX CHOCOLATE CAKE

[makes 1 (9 x 13–inch) cake]

Chocolate cake was a weekly staple in our house when I was growing up, my mother's version the only one my father claimed he cared for; he called it his "Vitamin-C." When he and my mother were courting—after he'd returned from World War II, at a time when the said tried-and-true way to a man's heart was through his stomach—she perfected chocolate cake with boiled, beaten fudge icing. My father's other cake edict was "No box cakes!" My grandmother hadn't been much of a scratch cook, so when cake mixes came into fashion she embraced them with great enthusiasm, something my chocolate-loving father and his six brothers were less than excited about.

After my parents were married, my mother baked a large, rectangular, one-layer chocolate cake frosted with hand-beaten fudge frosting every Sunday night, and every morning during the workweek she put two generous, waxed paper–wrapped squares of it in his lunch pail: one for his midmorning coffee break, the other for dessert after lunch. At 3:15 every afternoon two smaller pieces—like the ones she'd pack with the kids' lunches—would appear on the kitchen table next to two coffee cups, and moments later my father would be coming in the back door, closely followed by my brother and me. By then the cake, in its aluminum rectangular tin with the slide-shut lid, was put well out of our reach; we might get those smaller squares in our lunch boxes, but not every day, and definitely not for our after-school snack.

· · ·

This moist, dense cake can be baked into two (9-inch round) layers or a dozen large or eighteen regular-sized cupcakes. The amount of frosting in the recipe that follows is sufficient to frost any of these versions.

8 tablespoons (1 stick) salted butter, at room temperature

¾ cup dark brown sugar

3 large eggs, beaten

1 teaspoon vanilla

3 (1-ounce) squares unsweetened chocolate, melted

2 cups cake flour

2 teaspoons baking soda

½ teaspoon salt

¾ cup whole milk, sour milk, or buttermilk

Boiled Fudge Frosting (recipe follows)　　　　>>

Chocolate Cake　With love Mom
Blanche Carpenter
2 cups flour (sifted)
3/4 c. milk

1/2 c butter
3 eggs (beaten)
3/4 c brown sugar
1 tsp. pure vanilla
3-1 oz squares of unsweetened chocolate (melted)
Preheat oven to 350°.
Cream butter well, add brown sugar, then cream some more; add vanilla and melted chocolate and mix until batter is smooth. Add the flour, then milk alternately - beginning and ending with flour. Bake in a 9X13 cake pan which has been greased and floured for 30-35 minutes

1. Preheat oven to 350 degrees; grease and flour a 9 x 13–inch cake pan. Use an electric hand or stand mixer to beat butter until light; add sugar and mix thoroughly. Add beaten eggs and continue mixing; add vanilla and melted chocolate and mix until batter is smooth.

2. Sift flour once, then resift with baking soda and salt. Beginning and ending with flour mixture, fold into batter alternately with the milk, in three additions. Pour into prepared cake pan, using a spatula to evenly spread batter to the sides of the pan.

3. Bake in the center of the preheated oven for 30 to 35 minutes or until a wooden pick inserted in the center comes out clean. Cool in pan to room temperature before frosting.

BOILED FUDGE FROSTING

[makes 3 cups]

My mother's frosting recipe calls for light corn syrup, which I've left in to make it as she did; it helps keep the cake moist. Some healthier alternatives are a simple syrup of four parts white sugar to one part water; honey, which is more nutritious but will make the frosting taste sweeter; bran syrup, one of the better alternatives, which can be difficult to find; or light molasses or agave nectar, both of which change the flavor substantially. Mom always used Hershey's unsweetened chocolate squares, which was pretty much the only option in the 1950s and '60s. I've made it with some of the higher-end unsweetened chocolates available today; Scharffen Berger, made in California by former wine makers, is one of my favorites.

3 cups white sugar

1 cup cold water

2 tablespoons light corn syrup

4 (1-ounce) squares
unsweetened chocolate, broken
in pieces

pinch salt, optional

2 tablespoons salted butter

½ teaspoon vanilla

1. Fill the bottom of a double boiler with just enough water so the top pan sits above and not in contact with the water. Place sugar in the top pan; stir in water to dissolve, followed by corn syrup. Add chocolate, clip a candy thermometer to the inside of the boiler top, and cook over medium heat—*without stirring*—until the mixture reaches 234 degrees. While the frosting is cooking, prepare an ice bath deep enough to reach to 2 inches below the pan's rim; place a trivet or large-mouth canning ring in the bottom to elevate the pan, allowing the water to fully circulate around; this will cool the mixture quickly and evenly.

2. When the frosting has reached the soft-ball temperature (234 degrees; see sidebar), remove to the ice water bath, setting pan on top of the trivet, and quickly stir in the salt and add the butter, leaving it to melt on its own. Let rest in the ice bath until the temperature has dropped to 115 degrees. Once cool, stir

>>

Boiled Icing Basics

Boiled icings are all about two things: patience and accuracy—seemingly opposites in some camps, but don't let that deter you. This frosting needs to be cooked without stirring until the mixture reaches the soft-ball stage (234–240 degrees) so that it will thicken to a proper spreading consistency when beaten. This basic candy-making technique results in, essentially, spreadable fudge.

You need to monitor the temperature with an accurate thermometer, and this is no job for an instant-read. If the temperature rises too fast, the chocolate will seize and you'll have very hard fudge instead of creamy chocolate frosting. An accurate candy thermometer that clips on the inside of the pan without touching the bottom is what you want, that and a strong stirring arm.

If you don't have the former, test for the soft-ball stage by dropping a spoonful of frosting into very cold water, then pinching it between your thumb and forefinger to see if a soft ball has formed; you should be able to remove the ball from the water and it should flatten when you set it on a surface. You'll need to start testing and retesting once the mixture has begun to boil (212 degrees), but watch carefully—*again, without stirring*—because at this stage the temperature will rise faster than it did before the mixture came to a boil. Immediately remove pan from the heat to an ice water bath in the sink when the temperature reaches 234 degrees or the soft-ball stage.

And if you don't have the latter, employ the help of a strong-armed teenager with the promise of payment in chocolate cake. It always worked with my brother.

in vanilla. Sit on a solid chair, cover your lap with an apron or a dish towel, and begin beating the fudge in an overhand motion with a wooden spoon; continue until it's thick enough to hold its shape when spread on the cake. Don't try to use a mixer: it won't develop the proper consistency.

3. To frost, place half of the frosting in the middle of the top of the cake while the frosting is still slightly warm, and start spreading to the sides of the cake with an offset icing spatula or a straight, flexible metal spatula, working in a light, quick back-and-forth motion. Don't put too much frosting on at first or use too much pressure: it will make tears in the tender surface of the cake. Spread remaining frosting evenly over the first layer. Slice and serve.

Cook's Notes: Serve cake plain or with a scoop of French vanilla ice cream.

Lumberjack and Miner's Favorite Cake

On the northernmost reaches of the early Iron Range, a trip to the nearest town might take a day in the summer and up to several in winter. Any provisions—especially food—needed to be bought in large, storable quantities before the snow got too deep and travel too difficult.

Toward the end of winter, housewives had to be creative with their cooking, especially when baking. When the cupboard was nearly empty, dried fruits, mainly apples and raisins, were used the most, often in loaf cakes. Boiling or soaking the fruit in warm water plumped them up, and the sweet water was used as the liquid to replace depleting supplies of sugar, honey, and molasses.

This recipe reportedly was brought from England in about 1912 by a couple who cooked at one of the lumber camps on the far eastern point of the Vermilion Range, near the beginning of the Gunflint Trail. The cake was said to be a favorite with the lumberjacks. It's certainly a testament to the Iron Range resourcefulness that pioneer Mother Hubbards needed to muster when their cupboards were truly bare.

HOMESTEAD CAKE

1 cut-up apple and 2 cups raisins, boiled, use juice and all

1 teaspoon soda

enough flour to make a stiff dough

1 teaspoon salt

½ teaspoon cinnamon

½ teaspoon cloves

2 eggs, if you have any

1 cup margarine or refined bear fat

Mix and place in large greased loaf pan (or 2 small ones) and bake for 1½ hours at 300 degrees.

DO NOT EVER USE CAKE FLOUR.

ILMAPUURO /
FINNISH CRANBERRY AIR PUDDING

[serves 3–4]

Sisu! Quite possibly the most important word in the Finnish vernacular, and one expressed with pride the length of the country—from the nomadic, Uralic-speaking Saami in the sparsely populated Lapland region above the Arctic Circle to the multilingual Finn-Swedes in the teeming cosmopolitan "Finnish Riviera" town of Hanko at the southernmost tip. *Sisu* is figuratively translated into English as "strength of will; determination; perseverance; acting rationally in the face of adversity; not momentary courage, but the ability to sustain an action against the odds." *Ilmapuuro* could've been called the perfect example of culinary *sisu* for Finnish immigrants: the use of a strong arm to make a light dessert when faced with heavy financial, ingredient, and seasonal constraints. Now that the few items needed to make *Ilmapuuro* are easily available, enjoy it as the *Suomalainen* did, as both a dessert pudding and a special occasion breakfast porridge.

. . .

Cranberries are a seasonal item—available late fall to early winter—but freeze well, offering some advantages. Juice is elicited during thawing, and it's the juice that is used; the pulp is discarded. With frozen cranberries, you can make *ilmapuuro* in the spring and summer, too. Traditionally *ilmapuuro* was made with semolina; today farina cereals, like Cream of Wheat or Malt-O-Meal, which are less dense when cooked are commonly used. The instant types don't work, so you'll still need a strong arm to beat the heaviness out and bring the lightness in; or you could use an electric mixer.

1 (12-ounce) package fresh cranberries

¾ cup white sugar

½ cup uncooked farina (see head note)

1 cup heavy cream

coarse-grained brown or Demerara sugar for garnish, optional

>>

*If using frozen cran-
berries, thaw directly
in the saucepan
before adding water
to determine the
amount of additional
water needed—if any—
for cooking.

1. Place cranberries in a large, stainless steel saucepan and add just enough water to cover;* bring to a boil and cook until cranberries burst. Strain, pressing down on fruit to extract 3 cups of juice.

2. Pour extracted juice back into the saucepan, place over high heat, and bring to a boil. Add sugar while stirring constantly. Slowly add farina, stirring constantly to break up any lumps; cook at a low boil 15 to 20 minutes, lowering heat as needed to keep from scorching. Remove from heat and pour into a large bowl.

3. Beat at high speed with an electric hand mixer until light colored and very fluffy—about 20 minutes—rotating the bowl every few minutes; or 30 minutes by hand with a wire whisk. Chill in refrigerator. Serve cold with heavy cream— unwhipped or whipped, as you prefer. Garnish with coarse sugar as desired.

Cook's Notes: *Though not traditional, other flavorings can be added. Try orange or lemon zest or some thinly sliced fresh gingerroot cooked with the cranberries; a few whole cloves or a small fresh bay leaf are other possibilities. All will remain with the fruit pulp when strained. Garnish the cream with a sprinkling of ground ginger and orange or lemon zest if desired.*

CUSTARD PIE
WITH GINGERSNAP-CRUMB TOPPING

[serves 6–8]

Old fashioned? Yes. Out of date? Definitely not. From downright homey to elegantly gilded, custard is the ultimate in universal comfort foods. Found in nearly every culture, its foundation components are the same: eggs, milk or cream, and a sweetening agent. Flavoring, consistency, and preparation technique are where the differences come in. Thin custards are used for dessert sauces, baked or steamed into puddings—unmolded or eaten directly from cups—or used as bases churned into ice cream. Thick custards fill pies and pastries and are eaten as puddings or frozen on their own.

Those three basic and relatively inexpensive ingredients were found in every larder, making it possible for a sweet dessert to be enjoyed in the largest and poorest of families. This was the case in my grandmother's home, where seven sons all came of age during the years of the Great Depression through World War II. A move from town out to the country provided Grandma with more than needed space for a large family; a few cows and chickens became an important support system to help feed her growing herd.

· · ·

A creamy, quiet custard is a great means to make individual, star ingredients shine. Other than the basics, only one or two other flavorings should be added, or the taste could become murky and the consistency compromised. The best pie is made by partially baking the shell, which is done faster and at a higher heat than suitable for a custard, which should be cooked slowly to produce a creamy texture. My grandma topped her custard pie with crumbs from the large batches of cake-like molasses cookies she always had on hand; I've changed it up with crumbs from my favorite: gingersnaps, or Spicy Swedish Ginger Thins (page 157).

Many people find making pie dough intimidating, but it is really very simple. The key to a flaky crust is working quickly and not overmixing so the fat stays as cold as possible. It can be very successfully made in a processor or with an electric mixer, but the ingredients tend to heat up faster than when mixed by hand. Trying it by hand initially will give you a good sense of what the mixture should look and feel like. The recipe below is for a single crust, but the ingredients can be increased straight across the board for multiple and double-crust pies. The dough freezes well, so make extra; tightly wrap individual rounds in plastic, and thaw overnight in the refrigerator for pie on the fly—more time eating and less time cleaning.

CRUST

1½ cups all-purpose flour

1½ teaspoons white sugar

½ teaspoon sea or kosher salt

4 tablespoons (½ stick) cold, unsalted butter, cut into small pieces

¼ cup very cold vegetable shortening, cut into small pieces

¼ cup cold water

CUSTARD

3 large eggs or 6 large egg yolks, at room temperature

½ cup white sugar

¼ teaspoon sea or kosher salt

2 cups whole milk or 1 cup milk and 1 cup light cream (half-and-half), at room temperature

1 teaspoon vanilla

½ cup finely ground gingersnap crumbs

>>

1. In a large bowl, combine flour, 1½ teaspoons sugar, and ½ teaspoon salt; mix well. Scatter the cold butter over the top and toss. Use your fingertips—or a pastry blender or two table knives—to rub or cut the butter into pea-sized pieces; toss to mix. Repeat with the chilled shortening.

2. Sprinkle half the water over the mixture and toss. Add remaining water a little at a time, quickly but gently working into the flour until a tender but cohesive dough is formed. Hand-worked dough often needs a little more water than that made in a processor or with an electric mixer.

3. Form dough into a ball, place on a lightly floured surface, and flatten into a ¾-inch-thick disk; turn so both sides are coated with flour. Wrap in plastic and place in refrigerator to rest for at least 1 hour or overnight.

4. Remove dough from refrigerator and place on a lightly floured surface, chilled if possible. Flatten a bit by pounding with the rolling pin, then turn dough over to flour both sides. Roll into a circle by pushing the rolling pin away from you in swift, single strokes of even pressure; don't bear down, and don't roll back and forth. At the far edge, lift the pin slightly to maintain an even thickness; rotate dough by one-quarter after a few strokes, turn over and repeat until you have a circle that is 1½ inches larger in diameter than your pie pan (8½ for a 7-inch tin; 10 ½ for a 9-inch tin). Drape over the rolling pin and unfold into the pie plate, gently pushing down around the bottom. Flute by pinching around the top edge with lightly floured fingertips or by pressing down with the tines of a dinner fork; lightly prick entire surface with the tines of a fork—don't pierce crust all the way through. Refrigerate 30 minutes.

5. Preheat oven to 425 degrees. Bake pie shell for 10 minutes; remove from oven and reduce temperature to 325 degrees. Meanwhile, make the custard.

6. Beat eggs until whites and yolks are well blended or yolks are light; add ½ cup sugar and ¼ teaspoon salt, mixing well. Stir in milk or cream, followed by vanilla.

7. Open oven and pull rack partway out; place par-baked crust in the middle. Slowly pour filling into crust and carefully slide shelf back in; close door and

bake for 10 to 15 minutes. Open oven, carefully slide rack out, and evenly sprinkle gingersnap crumbs over the top. Continue baking for another 15 minutes or until edges of custard are set and middle is still slightly soft.

8. Remove from oven and place on a cooling rack; the entire pie will set as it cools. Serve at room temperature.

Mincemeat

Early Iron Range settlers found a ready food source in the area's abundant wild game, which was a good thing because most had neither the time nor the means to raise the livestock needed to feed their fast-growing families.

Venison, moose, and the occasional bear most often filled the need for animal protein, but all had strong, unappealing gamey flavors and were chewy and tough. Making mincemeat—the traditional Old English Christmas holiday pie filling of wild meats combined with dried fruits, nuts, molasses, suet, and brandy, whiskey, or wine—was a good way for early settlers to mask some of those unpalatable elements. Along with overriding the gamey flavor, the alcohol acted as a preservative in a time and place where canning and refrigeration were not yet everyday options.

Eventually, mincemeat would morph into a sweeter, more fruit-based filling for pies and tarts, with little or no meat or suet in the mix. It's now commonly found in bakery pies at Christmas or in the baking aisle of most grocery stores. There are still some hard-core deer hunters in the north woods who make their own venison mincemeat every fall; you just need to know how to track them.

Blueberry pie eating contest, Oliver Iron Mining company picnic

GRANDMA CARLSON'S BLUEBERRY CRUNCH

[serves 6]

Grandma Carlson was one of the tiniest grandmas I knew. She blamed her size on her desire to be a child again, and she almost was—in both respects. She was our next-door neighbor, and by the time I was eight and nine, I was almost eye to eye with her when we'd meet while picking lilacs from the bushes that separated our houses. I was tall for my age, but not excessively so. She had a great sense of humor and was always interested in what we were doing for school projects and what our plans were for summer vacation. She always bought Girl Scout cookies from several of us on the block. Not that she had to.

She baked cookies herself, for us and for her granddaughters, who lived a little ways outside of town but were frequent visitors on weekends during the school year and for weekday overnights in the summer. There was a big berry patch out at their house—raspberries, strawberries, and blueberries—and when they'd come to town in the summers, they'd bring whatever berries were ripe to their grandmother, and she would make jam. That was mostly with the strawberries and raspberries. The blueberries were for pie, muffins, and crunch. In late July, when the blueberries were ripe, she'd let us know when something was baking and when it would be done so my mom and I would be sure to come over while it was still warm. While my mom was gathering up some ice cream or something to "go with," I was already seated on the top step of Grandma Carlson's gray, lattice-enclosed porch five or ten minutes before she took the crunch out of her tiny, apartment-sized oven. I didn't need a second invitation.

Grandma Carlson passed away when I was twelve years old. It made me sad to know I would never again be greeted by those laughing blue eyes that in the end I had to stoop to look into. Before she died, she gave me her blueberry crunch recipe, written in her spidery hand on a little recipe card embossed with the words, "From Grandma's Kitchen . . . with LOVE." The card was misplaced long ago, but the recipe is baked into my memory.

BOTTOM

2 tablespoons all-purpose flour

¼ teaspoon kosher or iodized salt

½ cup white sugar

1 pint fresh blueberries, rinsed

zest of 1 lemon

2 tablespoons fresh lemon juice

TOP

1 cup rolled oats

1 cup all-purpose flour

½ cup firmly packed brown sugar

½ teaspoon kosher salt

½ teaspoon vanilla

16 tablespoons (2 sticks) unsalted butter, chilled

SERVING

whipped cream

1. Preheat oven to 350 degrees. Lightly grease an 8-inch square or 7 x 11–inch pan. Place 2 tablespoons flour, ¼ teaspoon salt, and ½ cup sugar in a medium bowl and stir together. Add blueberries and stir; sprinkle on lemon zest and stir; drizzle lemon juice over all and stir again. Pour into prepared pan.

>>

2. Using the same mixing bowl, combine oats, 1 cup flour, ½ cup brown sugar, and ½ teaspoon salt. Sprinkle vanilla over dry ingredients and mix. Cut each stick of butter into 8 pieces, and work into the dry mixture by hand, a few pieces at a time, until it resembles cornmeal. Sprinkle over the top of the blueberries, evenly covering the surface up to the sides of the pan. Bake for 30 to 40 minutes, until browned, with blueberry mixture bubbling up. Serve warm with heavy or unsweetened whipped cream.

NOODLE KUGEL PUDDING

[serves 8–10]

It's eaten on the Sabbath, for Shabbat. It could be breakfast. It could be dessert. It could be dinner. "It might sound strange, with the cereal, cinnamon, and brown sugar," said Tessy Oxman, "but this is very good with fish!"

. . .

Custards and other recipes with large amounts of liquid and eggs always turn out better when baked in glass dishes; they conduct heat faster and more evenly than metal pans. They also hold heat longer and can double as serving dishes on a buffet.

TOPPING

1 cup cornflakes or raisin bran, crushed

1 teaspoon cinnamon

½ cup firmly packed light brown sugar

PUDDING

8 ounces (¼-inch-wide) egg noodles

8 ounces cream cheese, at room temperature

8 tablespoons (1 stick) salted butter, at room temperature, plus more for baking dish

4 large eggs, beaten

2 cups whole milk, warmed

1. Preheat oven to 350 degrees. Bring a large pot of water to a boil and add a dash of salt. While water is heating, combine topping ingredients in a bowl and set aside. Boil the noodles until barely undercooked; drain in a colander, shake well

to remove all water, and place in a large bowl. While noodles are cooking, heavily butter the sides and bottom of a 9 x 13–inch glass baking dish or a similarly sized oval casserole.

2. Using an electric hand mixer or a rotary beater, beat the cream cheese and butter until fluffy; blend in beaten eggs until mixture is smooth, followed by the warm milk. Pour over noodles, mix well, and turn into the buttered dish. Spread topping mixture evenly over noodles, making sure to cover at the edges. Bake for 40 to 60 minutes, until a thin knife inserted in the center comes out clean.

3. Cut in squares and serve while still warm.

Cook's Notes: *Kugel reheats beautifully; tightly wrap leftovers and refrigerate. To reheat, place squares in the top of a double boiler over simmering water for 5 to 10 minutes, covered. Or put in a shallow dish, lightly cover with plastic wrap, and reheat in the microwave on medium heat for 2 to 3 minutes.*

COOKIES

SPICY SWEDISH GINGER THINS

[makes 60 thinly sliced cookies]

The annual Christmas bazaars across the Range were showcases for some of the more talented bakers in the region; to call them casual, friendly competitions would be an understatement in some towns and congregations. Some women were so well known for their special ethnic bread, pastry, or confection that people from other churches would make a point to be at the holiday sales where these coveted baked goods were being sold. The classic, traditional cookies, cakes, and breads always sold out first; smart shoppers arrived early.

One of these stellar bakers was Helga Lindvall, a member of First Lutheran Church in Hibbing. Her spicy ginger cookies eclipsed the competition; she must have made hundreds every year. Helga was not competitive, and she willingly shared her recipes with anyone who asked. She and my mother were in the same church circle and spent quite a bit of time making and serving church lunches over the years, during which many recipes were exchanged, including for her Spicy Swedish Ginger Thins.

Helga and her husband, Bill, were immigrants from different parts of Sweden who had come to America as children and met and married in Minnesota. These, she said, were his favorite cookies to have every day with his coffee.

* * *

These cookies come with a slightly crunchy exterior coating of the same spice mixture used to flavor the dough, giving them an extra zing. Sifting the flour through a fine mesh sieve or strainer makes for a delicate texture; if you don't have either, pass through a regular sifter twice.

This generous recipe yields sixty cookies, but you don't need to bake them all at once. Shape the dough into several logs and store one or two, tightly wrapped in plastic, in the refrigerator or freezer to slice and bake whenever you wish.

⅔ cup (1 stick plus 2⅔ tablespoons) salted butter, at room temperature

¾ cup firmly packed dark brown sugar

2 tablespoons cinnamon

1 tablespoon plus 1 teaspoon ground ginger

1 tablespoon ground cloves

2 teaspoons ground white pepper

2½ cups all-purpose flour

1 teaspoon baking soda

¼ cup boiling water

1 tablespoon white sugar

1. In a large bowl, beat the softened butter and brown sugar until light and fluffy. In a small bowl, mix the cinnamon, ginger, cloves, and white pepper. Add half the spices to the butter-sugar mixture and mix until well blended; set aside remaining spices. Sift measured flour through a fine-mesh sieve onto a piece of parchment or waxed paper about 18 inches long. Put baking soda into a liquid measuring cup and add boiling water to the ¼-cup mark; stir to dissolve.

2. Wrap the parchment around the flour, shake half over the butter-sugar mixture, and fold in with a rubber spatula. Add half of the baking soda water and stir in; shake remainder of the sifted flour over and fold in (reserve parchment), then stir in remaining baking soda water to form a stiff dough with a smooth, satin-like appearance. If dough is too stiff or seems too dry, add more hot water

1 tablespoon at a time. Place dough on the reserved parchment and spread down the middle. Tightly roll the parchment lengthwise around the dough so it spreads into a uniform half-dollar-size cylinder; you may need a second sheet of parchment. Refrigerate at least 30 minutes.

3. Preheat oven to 375 degrees. Line one—or several—flat baking sheets with parchment. Mix reserved spices with 1 tablespoon white sugar. Slice some—or all—of the chilled dough into ⅛-inch-thick rounds, dip in the reserved spice mix, and turn to coat. Place about half an inch apart on lined baking sheets, and bake for 8 to 10 minutes, until lightly browned. Cool on a wire rack; store in a tightly covered container for up to several weeks.

Cook's Notes: *These are great crumbled up as toppings for streusels, sprinkled over puddings (see custard pie, page 150) or sweet sauces (especially rhubarb, page 139), or even mixed in bread crumbs seasoned with some onion powder to coat pork cutlets or chops.*

PRASTEKRAGAR / SWEDISH CLERGYMAN'S COOKIES

[makes several dozen cookies]

Our diminutive neighbor, Mrs. Carlson, who was a great baker (see Grandma Carlson's Blueberry Crunch, page 154), kept tins of these cookies in her kitchen pantry, always ready to offer drop-in company along with a cup of coffee. They're the classic Scandinavian cookie, rich and buttery, warmly spiced with cardamom and ginger.

• • •

The shape of this cookie is meant to mimic those high, frilly white collars worn by the jowly, stern-faced Protestant Scandinavian clergymen in the nineteenth century—the ones who looked like they could use some spicing and sweetening up. The dough can be refrigerated overnight; let it sit at room temperature for a few minutes, about as long as it takes the oven to come to temperature, before rolling out. These are nice to serve with tea or at coffee klatches.

>>

4 cups all-purpose flour

1 cup white sugar

1 teaspoon sea or kosher salt

½ teaspoon ground cardamom or ginger or a combination, optional

2 heaping teaspoons baking powder

¼ teaspoon baking soda

4 tablespoons (½ stick) unsalted butter, chilled and diced

¼ cup vegetable shortening, chilled and diced

2 large eggs

¾ cup heavy cream or half-and-half

1 teaspoon vanilla

confectioners' sugar glaze (page 35), with ½ teaspoon ground cardamom or ginger or a combination stirred into icing, optional, thin enough to coat top edge and sides of collar without running off

1. Preheat oven to 350 degrees. Line several unrimmed baking sheets with parchment or lightly grease. Sift flour, sugar, and salt into a large bowl. Place spices (if using), baking powder, and baking soda into sifter and add to the sifted flour; stir with a wire whisk to combine. Use your fingers or a pastry blender to work chilled butter and shortening into flour mixture as you would for a pie crust.

2. Beat eggs until well combined; add cream and vanilla. Gradually stir liquid ingredients into dry ingredients; do not overmix. Place dough on a lightly floured surface, and roll out into a square ⅛ inch thick. Cut into strips ¾ inch wide and 3 inches long. Make 8 or 10 small cuts along the length about halfway through the width of the dough.

3. Using a flexible metal spatula, transfer to the prepared baking sheets, spacing evenly and curving each piece into a crescent, cut side up. Bake in the center of the oven until golden brown, about 10 to 12 minutes. Remove to a wire rack set on a baking sheet or pastry board. When almost cool, frost top edges with just enough icing so that it flows down but stays on the sides of the collar.

GRANDMA FIORI'S BISCOTTI

[makes 36 biscotti]

This recipe came to me from Carmela Fiori's daughters, Jackie and Olivia, who said their mother made them all the time. They were a family favorite, especially with their dad, Quentin, who had grown up eating them. The recipe was his mother's; she gave it to Carmela when they were first married. Grandma Fiori wanted to make sure her new daughter-in-law knew how to make them, too. She didn't have to worry: Carmela turned out to be one of the best cooks in town.

• • •

Seasoning the almonds with sugar, anise seed, and salt while still hot from the oven will intensify the flavoring of the biscotti. Use a good couverture-type chocolate in the sauce for a smooth, solid coating that is rich in taste without any waxy undertones; sprinkle a pinch of coarse sea salt over the warm chocolate to pick up the crunchy-salty almond notes in the biscotti.

2 cups all-purpose flour

2 teaspoons baking powder

½ teaspoon baking soda

¾ cup sliced blanched almonds

¾ cup white sugar

1 tablespoon plus 1 teaspoon whole anise seed, crushed

¼ teaspoon kosher or coarse sea salt

3 large eggs

2 teaspoons almond extract

10 tablespoons (1¼ sticks) salted butter, melted

milk, optional

Chocolate Coating (recipe follows)

1. Preheat oven to 300 degrees. Place flour, baking powder, and baking soda in a large bowl, and stir together with a wire whisk; set aside. Spread almonds evenly on a rimmed baking sheet; place in oven to lightly toast, about 5 minutes; watch the pan so they don't get too brown. Combine white sugar, crushed anise seed, and salt in a small bowl. Add warm almonds to sugar mixture, stir to coat, and fold into the flour mixture.

2. In a separate bowl, beat the eggs with a whisk and then add the almond extract, followed by the melted butter, whisking constantly. Add eggs to flour,

>>

stirring with a large spoon or rubber spatula until blended. The dough should be moist and pliable; if it's too dry, work in a teaspoon or more of warm water. Pat into a ball, cover, and refrigerate at least 30 minutes or overnight.

3. Preheat oven to 350 degrees. Remove dough from refrigerator to a lightly floured work surface, pat into a square, and cut into quarters. Roll each into a 3 x 6–inch rectangle, ½ to ¾ inch thick. Place portions ¾ inch apart on an ungreased baking sheet and brush tops with milk (if using). Bake in the center of the preheated oven for 25 to 30 minutes; watch carefully so the dough doesn't over brown, rotating baking sheet as needed. Remove from oven and cool slightly.

4. When cool enough to handle, use a metal spatula to transfer rectangles from the baking sheet to a cutting surface. With a serrated knife, slice each at an angle into ½- to ¾-inch-thick pieces; place biscotti on the ungreased baking sheets, cut sides down, and return to oven for 7 minutes; turn pieces over and bake another 7 minutes. Remove from oven, transfer from the baking sheet to a cooling rack that has been placed over a large sheet of parchment or waxed paper, and cool to room temperature. Prepare Chocolate Dipping Sauce.

5. Quickly dip one flat side of each biscotti in the warm chocolate, coating just the surface and not the sides. Place on the cooling rack, chocolate side up, and let topping harden. Stack in tightly covered tins or plastic containers; store at room temperature.

Cook's Notes: *The biscotti will harden in a day or two but are still good dipped in milk, coffee, or red wine.*

CHOCOLATE COATING

2 tablespoons unsalted butter	8 ounces semisweet or bittersweet chocolate, chips or cut in small pieces (see head note page 146)

1. Place butter in the top of a double boiler over simmering water. When butter is almost melted, begin adding chocolate pieces a few at a time, stirring until melted. Adding the chocolate in steps while stirring will make a smooth sauce that won't separate.

2. Remove the double boiler from the heat, but keep the top pot over the hot water in the bottom, stirring to keep the chocolate smooth and fluid. Dip the biscotti following the directions above.

BOB'S FRIDAY NIGHT FIGHT FUDGE

[makes 1 pound]

Friday nights my father and I made fudge, a tradition carried from the time he was a child, the second oldest of seven brothers. During the 1920s through the Depression years of the 1930s, my dad, his older brother Lew, and their third brother Ross would make short work of the supper dishes so they could get the fudge made. Times might've been tough, but there were always a few cups of sugar and enough unsweetened bits of chocolate for a batch of fudge. The boxing matches at Madison Square Garden were broadcast on the radio at eight o'clock every Friday night, and my dad and his brothers were faithful listeners and fans. Schoolwork could wait until Saturday or Sunday, but when the fights came on, they had to have fudge.

Most nights during the 1950s Dad headed out to his garage workshop after supper to tinker on one project or another. But on Friday nights, he occupied himself with the newspaper in the living room while my mother and I did the dishes and got the kitchen tidied up. The fights at Madison Square Garden would be on TV at eight o'clock. Projects could wait until Saturday or Sunday; we were faithful fans, and we had to have fudge.

* * *

I believe Dad got his recipe from the back of the box of unsweetened chocolate squares, though I'm not certain. I never saw him consult a cookbook or recipe card. You'll need a heavy-bottomed saucepan with a tight-fitting lid, a reliable candy thermometer, a good watch, and your dad's strong and steady forearm.

1 cup whole milk

2 cups white sugar

pinch salt

2 (1-ounce) unsweetened chocolate squares, broken into pieces

2–3 tablespoons salted butter, plus more for the pan

1 teaspoon vanilla

Optional ingredients:

½–1 cup chopped nuts

½ cup peanut butter, slightly warmed

coarse or flaked sea salt

1. Place milk in a large, heavy-bottomed saucepan and bring to a boil; remove from heat and stir in sugar and salt until dissolved. Add chocolate pieces and stir until melted.

2. Return pan to the heat and bring to a boil. Cover and cook for 2 to 3 minutes; the steam will dissolve any sugar crystals that form on the sides of the pan.

3. Remove lid, reduce heat, and cook without stirring until the soft-ball stage—234 degrees—registers on a candy thermometer. Keep an eye on the thermometer: the temperature will rise slowly at first, then come up suddenly. A pattern of small bubbles getting pulled into large bubbles on the surface will appear as the temperature is getting close. While chocolate is cooking, fill the sink or a large pan or bowl with ice water; evenly butter the sides and bottom of an 8-inch square pan.

4. When the mixture reaches 234 degrees, quickly but carefully remove from heat, keeping the liquid chocolate level in the pan. Place in the ice water bath and cool undisturbed until temperature drops to 110 degrees; the bottom of the pan should be cool to the touch. The mixture will become very smooth and shiny as it settles.

5. Remove from the water bath and stir in the butter with a large spoon; beat hard for a few seconds, add vanilla, and begin to beat vigorously—and constantly—until the mixture loses its sheen; the fudge should cling to the spoon without dripping. This is best done in a seated position, the pan in your lap held firmly with your non-stirring hand.

6. Quickly stir in nuts or peanut butter (if using); pour the fudge into the prepared pan, spreading to the sides and leaving a swirled texture on the top. Sprinkle on salt (if using). Score or cut into pieces before fudge hardens. Store at room temperature, covered with plastic wrap.

TESSY'S CARAMELS

[makes about 2 pounds]

At ninety-one years old, a body might want to slow down a little, but that's definitely not what Tessy Oxman has in mind for the moment. Besides having been a recognized master bridge player for many years—and she's still got game—she's long been acknowledged as a master cook among her peers—and she's definitely still on top of her game there, too. When I visited this engaged and engaging nonagenarian to talk about her early years in Hibbing, she generously shared more than memories about her family's food history and her early culinary interests, gifting me a jar of her famous strawberry jam, made the previous summer, and a jar of peach marmalade she'd made several months earlier. It was one of the best—and prettiest—preserves I've ever had, with beautiful colors, luxurious texture, and sublime taste.

· · ·

To ensure soft caramels, a candy thermometer is a good tool to invest in, and high-quality, real vanilla is a must. Tessy recommends vanilla from Madagascar for its deep, rich flavor. These days she buys precut candy wrappers instead of bothering with cutting squares out of waxed paper. "Those are too much trouble. Just go on the Internet and you'll find some there," she says.*

*To make your own, fold several lengths of waxed or parchment paper and cut into a few dozen 3½ x 4-inch pieces.

1–2 tablespoons unsalted butter, at room temperature

16 tablespoons (2 sticks) salted butter

2¼ cups firmly packed light brown sugar

pinch kosher or sea salt

1 cup light corn syrup

1 (12-ounce) can sweetened condensed milk (Carnation)

1 teaspoon vanilla (see head note)

1. Use softened butter to generously grease the bottom and sides of a shallow, square (8 x 8–inch) dish. In a deep, heavy-bottomed, 2-quart saucepan, slowly melt the 2 sticks of butter; add the brown sugar and salt, stirring until dissolved. Slowly add corn syrup and sweetened condensed milk and bring to a very slow boil, stirring constantly. Keep stirring while maintaining the boil to prevent scorching on the bottom. Hook a candy thermometer on the side of the pan—

>>

make sure the tip doesn't touch the bottom—and cook to 235 degrees, about 15 to 16 minutes. Watch the thermometer closely as the temperature goes up and remove from the stove immediately or the caramel will overcook.*

2. Add vanilla and stir until the caramel is smooth and glossy. Pour into the buttered pan, cover with plastic wrap or waxed paper, and let sit at room temperature 8 hours or overnight.

3. Line a baking sheet or other flat surface with a length of waxed or parchment paper. Using a teaspoon dipped in hot water, scoop portions of caramel out onto the paper, leaving a space between each; if the caramel begins to soften too much, place baking sheet in refrigerator for a few minutes. When all the caramel is portioned, lay out as many candy wrappers as will fit on a counter or tabletop. With clean, lightly buttered fingers, place a piece of caramel in the center of each; cover all squares before wrapping. Wash and dry your hands, and begin wrapping caramels by overlapping the longer sides and tightly twisting the ends; this will shape the soft caramels.

4. Store in a tightly covered container in the refrigerator or other cool area.

Cook's Notes: *Many of our mothers used the traditional liquid candy thermometers, but these are made of glass and can lose their accuracy over time. You can test the thermometer by hanging it inside a pot of boiling water without touching the bottom and monitoring the temperature for 10 full minutes, which tells you what temperature the boiling point (212 degrees) is for your thermometer. Then, adjust your recipes accordingly. Or buy a digital or coil-spring "dial" thermometer, both of which give faster, more accurate readings.*

RØMMEGRØT /
NORWEGIAN CHRISTMAS PORRIDGE

[serves 8–10]

The traditional holiday dessert in Norway is a porridge of thickened, boiled cream and milk under a coating of butter and cinnamon-sugar. Rich, warm, and wonderfully comforting, *Rømmegrøt* is the perfect thing to eat before bedtime on a chilly Christmas Eve.

• • •

The name translates literally into English as "sour cream porridge," and many recipes call for high-fat sour cream, but this one is made with heavy sweet cream. Most commercial sour creams are not high enough in fat and also contain stabilizers and gelatins which cause the cream to separate when boiled. To make your own stabilizer-free sour cream, heat 1 cup of heavy cream to 95 degrees, whisk in 2 tablespoons of buttermilk, cover, and let sit at room temperature for 8 hours or overnight.

2 pints heavy cream

⅔ cup all-purpose flour

1 teaspoon sea or kosher salt

2 tablespoons white sugar

2 cups whole milk, heated almost to boiling (to 210 degrees)

2 teaspoons cinnamon mixed with 1 tablespoon white sugar

1. In a heavy-bottomed saucepan, bring cream to a boil, stirring slowly with a large spoon so it doesn't burn on the bottom. Continue boiling and stirring for 15 minutes; remove from heat. Sift flour over cream while beating constantly with a wire whisk; stir in salt and sugar.

2. Return to low heat, whisking constantly. As butter rises to the top, skim to a glass measuring cup to keep warm for serving. Once butter is skimmed, remove pan from heat, stir in heated milk, and beat until smooth.

3. Portion into ceramic or glass dishes, top with reserved butter, and sprinkle with cinnamon-sugar. Serve warm.

RIISIPUURO / RICE PUDDING

[serves 6–8]

Rice puddings are a cultural commonality, eaten everywhere for almost every need, from the symbolic first taste of real food given to an infant to the universal palliative for the ill and aging. But those are served plain and unadorned. Celebration recipes abound with sweet additions and spices, some with raisins or orange, some with ginger, cinnamon, or cardamom, some with dates or pistachios, and many with a whole almond tucked inside, symbolizing an upcoming year of good fortune for its lucky finder.

• • •

At Christmas in Finland, *Joulupuuro* (Yule porridge) gets equal consideration as a comfort food (*lohtupuuro*), especially at a time when even the promise of good luck can't drive away the guarantee of the long, cold, dark days ahead.

1 cup white rice, rinsed	½ cup plus 2 teaspoons white sugar
5 cups whole milk	½ cup sliced unblanched almonds
½ teaspoon salt	
4 tablespoons [½ stick] salted butter, melted, plus more for dish	1 teaspoon cinnamon
	1 whole blanched almond
3 large eggs	light cream, optional

1. Fill the bottom of a double boiler with just enough water so the top pan sits above and not in contact with the water. Place rice in the top pan with milk, salt, and 4 tablespoons butter; cook over simmering water until barely tender, 1 to 1½ hours, stirring several times until milk has been absorbed. Beat eggs in a large bowl, add ½ cup sugar, and beat until thick. Butter a 2-quart glass baking dish or casserole. Preheat oven to 350 degrees.

2. When rice is ready, stir into the eggs and sugar until well mixed and pour into the buttered casserole dish. Combine sliced almonds, cinnamon, and 2 teaspoons sugar, reserve a pinch of the mixture, and sprinkle remainder evenly over the top. Bake for about 1 hour, until the pudding has set but is not firm. Remove from oven—make sure no one is watching when you do—and tuck the

whole almond in, then smooth pudding over your fingermark and cover with the reserved pinch of cinnamon-sugar.

3. Serve hot right from the oven, warm or at room temperature, or even chilled, with the light cream (if using) poured over the top.

Cook's Notes: *This is especially good, and comforting, with warmed Mormor's Rhubarb Sauce (page 139) and a few Spicy Swedish Ginger Thins (page 157) on the side.*

TESSY OXMAN'S LEMON MERINGUE PASSOVER SCHAUM TORTE

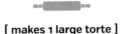

[makes 1 large torte]

Tessy says, "I always make this for Passover because there isn't any flour in it. You can make it ahead and freeze it, too. Just don't put the whipped cream on the top until you want to serve it. And it doesn't have to be completely thawed, either, which is good when you need something in a hurry; it's delicious as a frozen dessert!"

MERINGUE

8 large egg whites, at room temperature*

2½ cups white sugar

1 teaspoon white vinegar

FILLING

8 large egg yolks, at room temperature

1½ cups white sugar

juice and zest of 1 lemon

TOPPING

1 teaspoon unsalted butter

½ cup slivered, blanched almonds

pinch kosher salt

1 cup heavy cream

pinch fine white sugar, optional

*Save yolks for use in filling.

1. Make the meringue bottom a day ahead. Preheat oven to 300 degrees. Beat the egg whites until stiff and fairly dry; gradually add the sugar, followed by the vinegar, and beat well. Pour into an ungreased 10-inch springform pan. Use the back

>>

of a large, stainless steel spoon to press an indentation around the top, pushing the side edge up slightly, leaving a thin, raised rim around the diameter. Bake for 40 minutes, then turn off oven and leave pan in oven overnight.

2. The next day, remove meringue from oven and run a thin, dry knife around the inside edge of the pan to loosen. Open the spring, carefully remove the ring—leaving meringue on the pan bottom—and transfer to a serving plate.

3. For the filling, beat room-temperature yolks until thick; gradually beat in sugar until mixture is light yellow. Stir in half the zest, reserving remainder for topping, and add lemon juice. Beat well, until all juice is incorporated. Transfer to a heavy-bottomed stainless steel pot and simmer over medium heat until thick, about 15 minutes, stirring constantly. Remove from heat and cover surface of filling with plastic wrap or waxed paper to prevent a skin from forming on the top; set aside or refrigerate to cool.

4. For the topping, melt butter in a small skillet over medium heat until just beginning to bubble; add slivered almonds, coat with butter, and cook, stirring constantly, until just lightly browned. Remove from heat, drain fat, and spread almonds on a pan or plate to cool. Mix a pinch of kosher salt with reserved lemon zest; add cooled almonds and toss to coat. Whip heavy cream until it stands in peaks; add a pinch of sugar if desired.

5. To assemble tart, carefully slide a thin, metal spatula between the meringue and pan bottom to loosen. Spread a thin layer of whipped cream over the indentation in the meringue. Spoon the lemon filling in the middle of the cream layer and use a rubber spatula to spread it to the meringue rim, leaving a slightly higher mound in the middle. Sprinkle almond–lemon zest mixture over the top. Use a long, thin-bladed knife to cut into wedges for serving.

Cook's Notes: Run the slicing knife under hot water to make clean, even slices through the filling and the meringue. You can make individual tortes, too; spoon meringue mounds directly onto a parchment-lined cookie sheet and make the indentations with the back of a moistened teaspoon. Make sure to leave space in between for expansion. Bake the smaller meringues at the same temperature as the large one but for half the time: 300 degrees for 20 minutes. Turn off oven and remove pan for 20 minutes to allow oven to cool a little; return pan to oven after waiting period and leave overnight. The next day continue as for the large torte.

ÄITI'S *MANSIKKA KERMAKAAKKU* / FINNISH WHIPPED CREAM CAKE WITH STRAWBERRIES

[serves 8–10]

My uncle Eric, my mother's oldest brother, was a baker. He got his start as an army cook during World War II, and after his discharge in the mid-1940s he began an apprenticeship at the Sunrise Bakery in Hibbing, alongside Vince Forti, son of founder Giuilio Forti. In the early 1950s he and my aunt Lila and their infant son moved to the west end of the Mesabi Range and set up shop in the small town of Bovey. Four more children, three girls and another boy, followed, and by the late fifties the little apartment above the Bovey Bakery and Café was filled with two future bakers, two café owners, and one cake decorator. The boys apprenticed at their father's side in the basement, where the production part of the bakery was located, and the girls worked alongside their mother in the café upstairs. The middle daughter eventually found her calling in cake baking and decorating, a proclivity likely inherited from her *isoäiti*—maternal Finnish grandmother—who was a dairy farmwife and a wonderful cook and baker.

With several dozen dairy cattle at her disposal, Gramma Suomu, or Äiti, as we all called her, was always making something delicious with milk and cream, beyond the standard Finnish staples like *viili,* a live-culture yogurt (page 50); *kirnupiimä,* buttermilk; and *juustoleipä,* "Squeaky" Cheese (page 104). At Christmas there was always an *unni kiisipuuro,* creamy rice pudding (page 168), but best of all was her *mansikka kermakaakku,* cream cake with wild strawberries, made in early summer when the cows were in pasture eating clover and when wild strawberries could easily be found across nearby fields.

. . .

Almost a combination of an angel food and a chiffon cake, this one's easier and better. The eggs aren't separated, and there is no oil except for the scant amount used to grease the tube or Bundt pan; the fat comes from whipped cream. Building on the original, made with triple-sifted all-purpose flour, this recipe uses cake flour in combination with ultrafine, or baker's, sugar, which is finer than regular granulated, for an even lighter texture. The ultra-pasteurized heavy whipping cream is more stable and holds its volume when baked. Ripe strawberries are a must, and if you're lucky enough to have a source of wild ones, all the better.

*Ultrafine sugar is also called baker's sugar, which is cane sugar with very fine granules. You can approximate your own by putting ½ cup regular sugar in a spice mill or mini-processor and pulsing for 10 seconds or until the sugar is the size you want. If your recipe calls for less than ½ cup, you'll still need to pulse more than required to avoid over-processing a small amount. If you don't have a spice mill or mini-processor, use a large processor: just increase the amount of sugar to get the right consistency for the small amount you need. Use excess sugar in cooking as normal.

1½ cups cake flour

2 teaspoons baking powder

½ teaspoon fine sea salt

1 cup ultra-pasteurized heavy cream

2 extra-large eggs, at room temperature

1 cup ultrafine sugar*

1 teaspoon vanilla

½ cup thinly slivered almonds, lightly toasted

confectioners' sugar

1 pint ripe strawberries, thinly sliced

1. Preheat oven to 350 degrees. Chill a large metal bowl and beaters. Lightly grease a 9-inch tube or Bundt pan with canola or another light oil; set aside. Sift cake flour after measuring; sift again with baking powder and sea salt onto a flexible cutting board or a sheet of parchment paper.

2. Place cream in chilled bowl and whip until full and stiff; set aside. In a separate bowl, beat eggs until pale yellow and creamy; slowly add sugar while beating on high until fluffy; stir in vanilla. Carefully fold eggs and sugar into the whipped cream. Roll the cutting board or parchment around the flour mixture and shake over egg-cream mixture while folding in.

3. Pour into prepared pan, leveling with the back of a rubber spatula. Bake in the center of the oven until the edges of the cake pull away from the sides and tube of the pan, 50–60 minutes. Cool in pan at room temperature for 10 to 15 minutes. Run a thin, flexible knife around inside edges of pan to loosen and invert on a cooling rack.

4. Carefully slide onto a serving platter; top with half of the toasted almonds and some sifted confectioners' sugar; garnish around edges with half of the sliced strawberries. Use a long, thin-bladed knife (see notes) to slice. Garnish individual pieces with remaining almonds and strawberries.

Cook's Notes: *Moistening the knife blade under very hot running water will make slicing the cake very easy and clean. A Bundt pan gives a nice outside texture to the cake, but using a tube pan with a removable bottom ensures a cleaner release, with less chance of damage to the cake's delicate, fine structure.*

Justina Valentini and family in front of family cafe, Chisholm, Minnesota

MRS. FEDONILLA (ROSE) VALENTINI'S
CASTAGNOLE / FRIED ITALIAN HONEY PASTRIES

[makes 36–72 pastries]

Castagnole, or chestnuts—the Italian take on fritters—were originally made to celebrate Fat Tuesday on the eve of the forty-day Lenten fast, but these deep-fried, honey-drizzled, chestnut-sized pastries can be enjoyed at other times of the year, too. Any number of versions can be found, some with Marsala or sherry; some with milk and butter; even some that are baked and lightly dusted with powdered sugar (a modern-day attempt at healthy *castgne?* For Fat Tuesday?!). Rose Valentini of Chisholm relies on a tried-and-true, old family recipe—one brought from Italy—to make hers.

. . .

The traditional flavors and texture associated with *castagnole* come from the inclusion of finely grated lemon zest and anisette, a quick deep-frying in "miracle fat"—good pure lard—followed by a drizzling of honey over the perfect, crisp exterior. Pop one of these chestnuts in your mouth, lick your fingers, and follow up with a sip of lightly chilled Moscato or vin santo. *Mangia, bevi e spassatela!*

6 large eggs, at room temperature	2 ounces (¼ cup) anisette liqueur
2 tablespoons white sugar	4 cups all-purpose flour, sifted, divided
2 tablespoons light olive oil	2 tablespoons baking powder
½ teaspoon sea or kosher salt	1 cup pure lard
zest of 1 lemon	honey

1. In a large bowl, beat eggs for 1 minute, until frothy; mix in sugar until well combined. Stirring constantly, add oil, salt, lemon zest, and anisette.

2. Resift 2 cups of the flour with baking powder and stir into wet mixture. Mound remaining dry flour on a cutting board, make a well in the center, and add wet mixture. Using a fork, gradually work dry flour from the inside of the well into the wet ingredients to form a dough that is workable with your hands. The dough will be soft. Knead swiftly, lightly oiling your hands as needed to keep dough from sticking. Cover with a dish towel or the bowl and let rest for at least 1 hour; or wrap in plastic and refrigerate for up to several hours.

3. Melt lard in a (1½–2 quart) heavy-bottomed saucepan or cast-iron skillet with high sides, heating until temperature reaches 350 degrees on a candy ther-

Long Live Lard!

Hurrah! Lard's heavy reputation as an "evil fat" has started to lift. In fact, by weight lard has more unsaturated fat and less saturated fat than an equal amount of butter, and it beats butter in the lower cholesterol category, too. It goes one better against vegetable shortenings and many margarines: lard contains no trans fat whatsoever.

Once considered a food of the impoverished, lard is making a comeback. Bakers and pastry chefs in the know seek out sources of pure leaf lard to use in sweet and savory pies. Grandma always said the only pie crust is a lard pie crust— and Grandma always did know best.

So, long live lard!

mometer. Line a rimmed baking sheet with paper towel and set near the stove but away from direct heat. Place the honey container in hot water to liquefy.

4. Remove dough from resting spot or refrigerator; divide into several pieces and use palms to roll out into long strips—½ to ¾ inch in diameter. Cut into similar-sized pieces, up to 1 inch, and roll or stretch into various shapes. Drop several at a time into the hot lard so they are covered in the melted fat without crowding; fry until golden brown, about 3 to 5 minutes, turning with the end of a fork to evenly color. Remove with a slotted spoon to the paper towel–lined pan. Repeat with remaining dough pieces.

5. Place drained *castagnole* on a platter or individual plates while still a bit warm, drizzle with honey, and serve.

Cook's Notes: *You can cut these any length you like, but the smaller ones—½ to 1 inch—will cook faster and more evenly and absorb less fat; they are also easier to eat right away because they won't be too hot to pop in your mouth. Oversize* castagnole *can hold pockets of hot fat that could burn the mouth if eaten too soon out of the fryer.*

An Italian Christmas Day

Justina Valentini and her family celebrated Christmas at home on Christmas Eve, and on Christmas Day they opened their restaurant, Valentini's Supper Club, to feed whoever came in wanting or needing food free of charge. The younger children assembled in the dining room as the "family choir," offering entertainment while the older children and the adults ate, drank, and shared their Christmas. At the end of the day, leftovers were packaged into meals and delivered to homebound people in town who needed food and had no family to provide for them.

LEMON-GLAZED GINGERBREAD

[makes 1 (8 x 8-inch) pan]

Gingerbread in its various renditions is one of the oldest, most universally embraced comfort foods in the history of modern humans, with citations as far back as 1000 CE Armenia. From there, crisscrossing its way across the Turkish empire into the Adriatic north to the Slavic countries, over to the Italian and Spanish peninsulas, further north through Europe up to Scandinavia, gingerbread eventually reached American shores with the earliest of immigrants beginning sometime in the 1500s. I daresay, gingerbread's culinary lineage reads a close parallel to that of the early twentieth-century Iron Range, where it could be found in small-town and mining location homes as far as the ginger-colored veins extended, on out into the hard-to-reach rural and wilderness areas of farmers, loggers, and homestead pioneers.

Lard, flour, molasses, salt, and honey were normal pantry and root cellar staples for those early settlers, as were butter and eggs, once they were able to afford cows and chickens. Spices, like ginger and cinnamon? Extras, like powdered sugar and lemons? In that location at that time? Sorry, those were out-of-reach exotics.

* * *

This dense, spicy-sweet gingerbread is given an update from those pioneer times with a lemon glaze applied during the final ten minutes of baking so it becomes infused into the gingerbread and gives a nice sheen to the top after it has cooled. Freshly squeezed lemon juice is a must. Cover first with waxed paper or parchment, then plastic wrap, and store at room temperature.

Gingerbread is the ultimate in post-dinner, pre-sleep comfort foods. It's rich, so serve in small, slightly warm pieces with some unsweetened whipped heavy cream. Mint tea and fuzzy slippers optional, but highly recommended.

GINGERBREAD

1 large egg, beaten

½ cup packed brown sugar

2½ cups all-purpose flour, sifted

1½ teaspoons baking soda

1 teaspoon ground ginger

1 teaspoon cinnamon

½ teaspoon finely ground white pepper

½ teaspoon sea or kosher salt

1 cup very hot water

½ cup light molasses

½ cup light honey

zest of 1 lemon

8 tablespoons (1 stick) unsalted butter, melted and cooled

GLAZE

1 cup confectioners' sugar, sifted

¼ cup freshly squeezed lemon juice

1. Preheat oven to 350 degrees; grease an 8 x 8–inch baking pan. Beat egg in a small bowl; add brown sugar and mix well. Sift dry ingredients (flour through salt) into a separate bowl. Measure hot water into a bowl and add molasses and honey, stirring to dissolve. Stir in lemon zest.

2. Place cooled butter in a large bowl and add sugar-egg mixture, beating well with a spoon or whisk. Stir in dry ingredients, alternating with the molasses-honey mixture, until well blended. Pour into prepared baking pan. Bake for 45 minutes on middle oven rack. Make the glaze by stirring together confectioners' sugar and lemon juice until smooth.

3. After 45 minutes, remove pan from the oven and use a dinner fork to poke holes evenly over the surface and three-quarters of the way into the gingerbread. Pour lemon glaze over the top, spreading with a spatula so it evenly penetrates the cake. Return to the oven and bake for another 10 to 15 minutes. Let cool almost to room temperature before cutting to serve.

Gust and Anna Canelake, in their Virginia, Minnesota, store, 1931

Over a Century of Hot Air

Canelake's is possibly the oldest business in the town of Virginia. In fact, it might be the oldest one of its kind in the entire state, and that's not just a lot of hot air. Founded by two Greek immigrant brothers, Canelake's has been soothing Iron Ranger sweet tooths for over a century.

Gust and Tom Canelake arrived in the United States in 1900, first settling in Chicago for five years before leaving the Windy City for the cold reaches of the Iron Range. They set up shop as the Virginia Candy Kitchen on one end of Chestnut Street in 1905, making them the oldest ongoing business in town, outside of the mining companies. Fifteen years and two moves later, they arrived at the location they've occupied for nearly a century; it was 1920, the same year that Gust's son John was born. John and brother Leo apprenticed with their father and uncle and eventually took charge of creating sweet memories for the better part of the twentieth century. Fresh and dried fruits and nuts were part of the original inventory, some in their natural state and others shrouded in coats of dark and milk chocolate. Upward of forty chocolate confections were eventually created, the most famous and loved being hot air, a Canelake original with a top-secret formula. Crisp, fluffy, light, airy, it remains one of the store's top sellers.

Health issues forced the brothers to retire in the 1980s, but not before they found a solid replacement in their apprentice, Jim Cina, who took over in 1983 and continues to uphold the quality and traditions set forth by Gust Canelake in 1905 and kept in place by his two sons for the better part of the following century.

All of Canelake's old-fashioned candies are available online, but you really should visit the Chestnut Street shop for the full aromatic experience.

CHAPTER 7

Everyday, Holiday, & Celebration Menus

*Toward the end of her story,
Linnea Eliason smiled and licked
her lips slightly, almost as if she were tasting
everything as she described it.*

THE AUTHOR

Historically, in poor cultures, the most prized and expensive foods were reserved for holidays and special occasions, such as weddings, births, and other rites of passage. The foods served were often traditional and specific to the event being celebrated. There were definite patterns in daily eating as well. Menus ranged from lavish, traditional, multi-course extravaganzas requiring strategic time management to simple, quickly prepared basics that incorporated minimal bites of savories and sweets or leftover tidbits extended and transformed for repeat performances.

Whether planning daily meals or special occasion feasts, aside from dietary considerations, the primary points to keep in mind are the inclusion of complementary tastes and textures. Some of the following menus are classic and others are a cross-cultural mix of many of the recipes included in the book—a number of which can be made in advance—with suggested, easy sides. For everyday eating, heavy dishes are typically accompanied by light fare, while the celebratory menus are somewhat expanded. These are just ideas for you to consider; follow your culinary instincts—they're usually the best guides—and create your own signature celebrations.

EVERYDAY BREAKFAST

Always: coffee or tea; fresh fruit or juice

ITALIAN FRITTATA (page 55) *or eggs poached, soft-boiled, or scrambled; breakfast meat of choice;* toasted **ITALIAN DAILY BREAD** (page 25), **SWEDISH** *LIMPA* (page 20), or **MILK BREAD** (page 27); **REFRIGERATOR BRAN MUFFINS** (page 12) *or lefse; butter, jam or jelly*

VIILI (page 50); **NORWEGIAN CHRISTMAS PORRIDGE** (page 167); *muesli;* toasted **SWEDISH** *LIMPA* (page 20); *butter, jam or jelly*

FRUIT SOUP (page 141); *VIILI* (page 50); *muesli;* **REFRIGERATOR BRAN MUFFINS** (page 12); *butter, jam or jelly*

Lightly fried last night's **JANSSON'S TEMPTATION** (page 85) or *GUBBEN RUNKA* (page 87); *soft-boiled or scrambled eggs;* **FINNISH HARDTACK** (page 18) *or lefse*

Great-grandmas Nonna (Virginia Ricci Forti) and Eva (Eva Barich Maras) fishing at Beatrice Lake, Minnesota, 1940s

BRUNCH, HOLIDAY, AND SPECIAL OCCASIONS

Always: coffee or tea, fresh fruit or juice

French toast; **FINNISH BISCUIT** (page 31); **CHALLAH** (page 37); **MILK BREAD** (page 27); **LINGONBERRY SAUCE** (page 53); *real maple syrup; butter; breakfast meat of choice*

SWEDISH PANCAKES (page 51); **LINGONBERRY SAUCE** (page 53) *or real maple syrup; butter; Swedish potato sausage or breakfast meat of choice*

NOODLE KUGEL PUDDING (page 156); *breakfast meat of choice;* **CHALLAH** (page 37); **GINGER-RHUBARB SCONES** (page 13); **REFRIGERATOR BRAN MUFFINS** (page 12); *butter, jam or jelly*

CRANBERRY AIR PUDDING (page 149), **NORWEGIAN CHRISTMAS PORRIDGE** (page 167), *or muesli;* **FRUIT SOUP** (page 141); *Swedish potato sausage or breakfast meat of choice;* **CREAMED HERRING SALAD** (page 112); **HARDTACK** (page 18); **HOT CROSS BUNS** (page 42)

ITALIAN FRITTATA (page 55) *or eggs poached, soft boiled, or scrambled; breakfast meat of choice;* **PANETTONE** (page 40); *JULEKAKA* (page 34); **HOT CROSS BUNS** (page 42); **CHALLAH** (page 37); **FINNISH BISCUIT** (page 31)

PEA SOUP (page 120); **CREAMED HERRING SALAD** (page 112) or **PICKLED PEPPERS** (page 97); **HARDTACK** (page 18); **SCANDINAVIAN LIVER PASTE** (page 110); *Havarti or farmer's cheese; butter; green salad with vinaigrette;* **HOMESTEAD CAKE** (page 148), **NORWEGIAN CHRISTMAS PORRIDGE** (page 167), or **LEMON-GLAZED GINGERBREAD** (page 176); or **SPICY GINGER THINS** (page 157) or **CLERGYMAN'S COOKIES** (page 159)

CHICKEN SOUP (page 116); **SLICED RADISH SALAD** (page 114) *or coleslaw with celery seeds and oil-vinegar dressing;* **ITALIAN ROLLS** (page 25) or **POTATO ROLLS** (page 29); **LEMON-GLAZED GINGERBREAD** (page 176), **SPICY GINGER THINS** (page 157), or **CLERGYMAN'S COOKIES** (page 159)

BEEF *MÔJAKKA* (page 118); **SLICED RADISH SALAD** (page 114), *cucumber salad,* or **BEET PRESERVES** (page 106); **HARDTACK** (page 18) or **POTATO ROLLS** (page 29); **APPLE STRUDEL** (page 142), **LEMON-GLAZED GINGERBREAD** (page 176), *iced molasses cookies,* or **SCHAUM TORTE** (page 169)

PASTIES (page 59); *cucumber salad or romaine or bitter green salad with vinaigrette;* **CUSTARD PIE** (page 150), *iced molasses cookies,* or **CARAMELS** (page 165)

PORKETTA SANDWICHES (page 68) on **ITALIAN ROLLS** (page 25); *coleslaw with celery seeds and vinegar-oil dressing;* **PICKLED PEPPERS** (page 97); **LEMON-GLAZED GINGERBREAD** (page 176), **RHUBARB SAUCE** (page 139) with cream, or **BLUEBERRY CRUNCH** (page 154)

SOUTH AMERICANS (page 61); *romaine or bitter green salad with vinaigrette;* **CRANBERRY AIR PUDDING** (page 149) or ***CASTAGNOLE*** (page 173)

SUPPERS (SERVED IN THE EARLY EVENING)

RAVIOLI (page 75); *romaine or bitter green salad with vinaigrette;* **BISCOTTI** (page 161), **SCHAUM TORTE** (page 169), or **CHOCOLATE CAKE** (page 144)

SWEDISH MEATBALLS (page 81); **LINGONBERRY SAUCE** (page 53); *mashed or boiled baby red potatoes; steamed or boiled carrots, peas, or green beans;* **SLICED RADISH SALAD** (page 114) *or cucumber salad;* **CUSTARD PIE** (page 150) or **SPICY GINGER THINS** (page 157)

SARMA (page 88); *boiled, steamed, or oven-roasted carrots;* **SWEET-SOUR CARAWAY RYE BREAD** (page 22) with butter; **APPLE STRUDEL** (page 142), **NORWEGIAN CHRISTMAS PORRIDGE** (page 167), or **LEMON-GLAZED GINGERBREAD** (page 176)

CRACKLING ROAST PORK (page 92); **SUGAR-BROWNED POTATOES** (page 126); *steamed or boiled buttered carrots with dill weed or oven-roasted squash;* **RHUBARB SAUCE** (page 139) with cream, **LEMON-GLAZED GINGERBREAD** (page 176), or **APPLE STRUDEL** (page 142)

SOME CELEBRATION DINNERS AND SUPPERS

Cucumber salad; **LUTEFISK** (page 79); *boiled baby red potatoes; buttered baby peas;* **SWEET-SOUR CARAWAY RYE BREAD** (page 22) with butter; **BEET PRESERVES** (page 106); **SCHAUM TORTE** (page 169) or **LEMON-GLAZED GINGERBREAD** (page 176); *slivovitz or aquavit*

STUFFED ARTICHOKES (page 103) or **ANTIPASTO** (page 98); *BRACIOLE* (page 83) or *roasted or grilled beef tenderloin;* **POLENTA** (page 123); **ITALIAN BEANS IN TOMATO SAUCE** (page 128); *CASTAGNOLE* (page 173) or **PANETTONE** (page 40); *dry red Italian wine or asti spumante*

"SQUEAKY" CHEESE (page 104); **SLICED RADISH SALAD** (page 114); **CRACKLING ROAST PORK** (page 92); **SUGAR-BROWNED POTATOES** (page 126); *steamed baby peas in mint cream sauce;* **LINGONBERRY SAUCE** (page 53) *or baby dill pickles;* **SPICY GINGER THINS** (page 157) or **CRANBERRY AIR PUDDING** (page 149); *aquavit or brandy*

LUNCHES (LATE-NIGHT SNACK)

Evening lunches were very common in a lot of cultures, coming at the ends of busy days and long weeks, when people might want just another little bite or two, something simple, not complicated, not overly spicy but warm and comforting. On the occasion of a planned late-night lunch, cooks often wanted to showcase one or two of their specialties. With sweet and savory leftovers almost always at hand, something quick and satisfying was easily pulled together.

Here then, a few suggestions for using up those last little bits from yesterday or the day before to lay out a bountiful late-night table with minimal effort.

A little something savory, with the last sip of wine...
Antipasto (page 98)
Sliced Radish Salad (page 114)
Bread Salad (page 115)
Jansson's Temptation (page 85)
Hardtack (page 18)
Creamed Herring Salad (page 112)
"Squeaky" Cheese (page 104)
Liver Paste (page 110)
Swedish Meatballs (page 81)
Lingonberry Sauce (page 53)
Milk Bread (page 27)
Potato Rolls (page 29)
Porketta (page 68)
Italian Rolls (page 25)

... and a little something sweet (and warm), to go with tea and maybe something a little stronger.
Swedish Rusks (page 15)
Cardamom Bread (page 31), toasted, with honey and butter
Fruit Soup (page 141)
Norwegian Christmas Porridge (page 167)
Lemon-Glazed Gingerbread (page 176)
Apple Strudel (page 142)
Rice Pudding (page 168)

ACKNOWLEDGMENTS

*P*utting a book together is like making a literary sandwich; multiple layers make up the whole. Starting with a bottom slice of bread, a foundation is laid down; then the filling—for which the sandwich is usually named——is put in place; and finally, a second slice of bread is pressed on top as the finishing touch. Without good, substantial bread on either side to hold the filling in place, a literary sandwich would be next to impossible—and not very desirable—to pick up and enjoy. My sincerest thanks to:

The collective team at the Minnesota Historical Society Press in St. Paul: Shannon Pennefeather, managing editor, for gently but firmly keeping me on task; Ann Regan, editor in chief, for taking the project on; Cathy Spengler, designer, and Judy Gilats, typesetter, for giving visual grace to my words; Nancy Root Miller, proofreader, and Ina Gravitz, indexer, for sorting them out; Alison Aten, publicity and promotions manager, Mary Poggione, sales and marketing director, and Jerry Bilek, sales manager, for enthusiastically spreading the word; and Pam McClanahan, director, who oversees this extraordinary group of individuals. Thanks also to the MNHS research library staff for filling my many document requests.

And on the Iron Range, Sue Godfrey, research specialist, and Christopher Welter, archivist, at the Minnesota Discovery Center in Chisholm; Leonard Hirsch, director, and Erika Larson, curator, at the Hibbing Historical Society; and Kathy Bergan, curator at the Iron Range Historical Society in Gilbert, all of whom went above and beyond in helping me with my research.

I need to thank a number of blended Iron Range immigrant, first-, and second-generation families, including the Gust and Anna Canelake family; Lewis and Jessie (Haigh) Carpenter family; the Ann Crnkovich family; the Anna Linnea Eliason family; the Quentin and Carmela Fiori family; the Guilio and Virginia (Ricci) Forti (Maras) family; the Eric and Anna (Baärs) Johnson (Carpenter, Suomo) family; the David and Tessy (Stein, Horowitz) Oxman family; the Sam and Maria Nicole Spadaccini (Cummings, Jacobson) family; the Justina Valentini family; the Joseph and Anna Vitali (Carpenter, Choidi) family; and my many second- and third-generation friends and family members—Iron Range and everywhere—who lent their eyes, ears, stories, research, recipes, taste buds, critiques, and encouragements as well. Hvala lijepa. Kiitos. Mille grazie. Todah. Tack så mycket. Dankeschön. Mnogo vam hvala. Tusen takk. Durdalada whye. Thank you.

Not as noticeable, but equally important, there needs to be a component on either side of the filling to bond it to the bread and keep the whole thing together.

Thanks to my binders, Trish Hampl (St. Paulite) and Cheryl Miller (Iowa Citian), both now Honorary Iron Rangers, who were there from start to finish.

INGREDIENT SOURCE LIST

Canelake's Home Made Candies
414 Chestnut Street, Virginia, MN
   55792
PHONE: 218-741-1557
ORDERS: 888-928-8889
WEB: www.canelakescandies.com
E-MAIL: canelakes1905@yahoo.com

Fraboni's Sausage Company
313 East Thirteenth Street,
   Hibbing, MN 55746
PHONE: 218-263-5074
WEB: www.frabonis.com
E-MAIL: mthune@frabonis.com

Sunrise Bakery
1818 Third Avenue East, Hibbing,
   MN 55746
PHONE: 218-263-4985
ONLINE ORDERS: 2810 Diane Lane,
   Hibbing, MN 55746
PHONE: 218-262-1219
FAX: 218-263-4305
ORDERS: 800-782-6736
WEB: sunrisecreativegourmet.com
E-MAIL: sales@sunrisebakery.com

Sunrise Deli
2135 First Avenue, Hibbing, MN
   55746
PHONE: 218-263-5713
WEB: http://www.sunrisedeli.net

Sunrise Market
864 Pierce Butler, St. Paul, MN
   55104
PHONE: 651-487-1913
*Sunrise products can be found in
over 250 grocery stores throughout
the Upper Midwest, at Twin Cities
metro co-ops, and at St. Paul, Minneapolis, and Des Moines farmers
markets.*

Valentini's Supper Club
31 West Lake Street, Chisholm, MN
   55719
PHONE: 218-254-2607
FAX: 218-254-2111
WEB: valentinissupperclub.com
E-MAIL: vcs2607@hotmail.com

Andrej's European Pastry
11691 Latick Road, Chisholm, MN
    55719
PHONE: 218-254-2520
WEB: www.poticawalnut.com
E-MAIL: andrejspotica@gmail.com

Black Bear Bakery
17 West Lake Street, Chisholm, MN
    55719
PHONE: 218-254-4772
WEB: www.blackbearbakery.com
E-MAIL: ionalutt@gmail.com

Buhl Water Company
400 Pennsylvania Avenue, Buhl,
    MN 55713
PHONE: 218-258-3258
WEB: www.buhl-water.com
E-MAIL: buhlwatercompany@
    yahoo.com

Koshar Sausage Kitchen
101 Broadway South Gilbert, MN
    55741
PHONE: 218-741-8827
E-MAIL: adamferkul@hotmail.com

Made on the Range
A site for established Iron Range
businesses of all kinds.
Iron Range Resources and
    Rehabilitation Board
4261 Highway 53 South, Eveleth,
    MN 55734
PHONE: 218-735-3000
WEB: www.madeontherange.com

BIBLIOGRAPHY

American Bicentennial Diamond Jubilee Cook Book. Chisholm Diamond Jubilee Committee, 1976. (Lumberjack and Miner's Homestead Cake)

Bernard Clayton, Jr. *The Complete Book of Breads.* New York: Simon and Schuster, 1973. (Panettone)

Cooking on the Range. A new edition of *The Old Country Cookbook: Iron Range Ethnic Food.* Chisholm, MN: Iron World Discovery Center, 2004. (*Pulla, Potica, Viili*)

Rhoda R. Gilman and June Drenning Holmquist, eds. *Selections from* Minnesota History, *A Fiftieth Anniversary Anthology.* St. Paul: Minnesota Historical Society, 1965. (epigraph page viii)

Hibbing Centennial Cookbook: 100 Years of Hibbing's Best Recipes. Hibbing Centennial Committee, 1993. (*Ilmapuuro*)

Shelley N. C. Holl and B. J. Carpenter. *The Minnesota Table: Recipes for Savoring Local Food Throughout the Year.* Minneapolis: Voyageur Press, 2010. (Potato Rutabaga Soufflé)

New Hot Off The Range. Compiled by the Jewish Women of the Hibbing-Chisholm Hadassah, 1981. (Challah, *Kreplach*)

Beatrice Ojakangas. *Scandinavian Feasts: Celebrating Traditions throughout the Year.* Minneapolis: University of Minnesota Press, 1992. (Crackling Roast Pork)

INDEX

PHOTO CREDITS

Come, You Taste was designed by Cathy Spengler and set in type by Judy Gilats. The typefaces are Malaga, Verb, and Cocktail Shaker.